**A KIPLINGER BOOK**

# Mom, Can I Have That?

## By Janet Bodnar

**KIPLINGER**
**TIMES BUSINESS**

RANDOM HOUSE

KIPLINGER
BOOKS

Published by
The Kiplinger Washington Editors, Inc.
1729 H Street, N.W.
Washington, D.C. 20006

**Library of Congress Cataloging-in-Publication Data**

Bodnar, Janet, 1949-
    Mom, can I have that? : Dr. Tightwad answers your kids' questions
about money / Janet Bodnar.
    Includes index.
    ISBN 0–8129–2754–0 (alk. paper)
    1. Children—Finance, Personal.    2. Parent and child.
HG179.B568    1996
332.024—dc20

96-4558
CIP

This publication is intended to provide guidance in regard to the subject matter covered. It is sold with the understanding that the author and publisher are not herein engaged in rendering legal, accounting, tax or other professional services. If such services are required, professional assistance should be sought.

First Edition. First Printing. Printed in the United States of America.

*Book designed by S. Laird Jenkins Corp.*

# Acknowledgments

Transforming any book manuscript into a finished product takes a team of editors, designers, artists, researchers and proofreaders. Transforming this manuscript into the polished product you hold in your hands took the skilled team of professionals at Kiplinger Books.

I am especially indebted to David Harrison, who had the original inspiration and made it work; to editor Jennifer Robinson, for her creativity and fresh perspective, and her never-failing encouragement; to Karmela Lejarde, Brent Johnson, Carol Mickey and Dianne Olsufka, for their diligent research, proofreading, checking and for their yeoman service in the clutch.

On a personal note, I'd like to say thanks to my parents, Edward and Irene Bodnar, and my sister, Priscilla Jackman, for being such loyal fans; to John, Claire and Peter, my in-house team of expert testers and advisers; and to my husband, John, for going through it all a second time.

Finally, a tip of the pen to Dr. Tightwad, the *real* champion of family values.

# Contents

# Introduction

By Knight A. Kiplinger
Editor in Chief
*Kiplinger's Personal Finance Magazine*

Here's a scary thought: Children's handling of money is learned more from their parents' *behavior* than from their parents' *advice.* Whatever you say to them, your kids will probably end up "doing as you do and not as you say." So the best education we adults can give our kids on the wise handling of money is to set a good example and hope they emulate it, now and in later years.

But let's get real. Whatever examples we try to set for our children—thrift, deferred gratification, the emptiness of acquisitiveness—there are plenty of other social forces tempting them with opposite messages. Peer pressure, commercials on TV, celebrity endorsements—they're all powerful antidotes to parental example.

Setting a good example isn't enough when you're facing a barrage of questions, demands and occasional whining from your kids. You need something more, and that something is what Janet Bodnar calls "the snappy comeback"—an answer that is clearly reasoned and clearly stated (and sometimes witty to boot).

As the mother of three children, Janet gets lots of practice handling the tough questions and real-life money issues that all parents face. She's also a collector of parental wisdom, and she has good channels for sharing this wisdom with others. Under the *nom de plume* of Dr. Tightwad, Janet's advice first appeared in 1992 in the pages of *Kiplinger's Personal Finance Magazine,* of which she is senior editor. There followed a best-selling book, *Kiplinger's Money-Smart Kids (And Parents, Too!),* a newspaper column syndicated by The New York Times Syndicate, and many television and radio appearances. In a few short years,

Janet Bodnar's Dr. Tightwad has become the Dr. Spock of money-smart childrearing.

This book is a veritable compendium of the toughest questions kids ask about money. All are accompanied by Dr. T's snappy comebacks and, even better, her prescriptions for curing stubborn cases of infectious materialism. These prescriptions are formulated with the help of professional experts—child development specialists, marriage counselors, financial pros—as well as real–life experts . . . the parents who field their kids' questions and come up with answers that really work.

Like Janet Bodnar, I am both a financial journalist and parent of three kids, and I've contributed a few case studies and suggested solutions to Dr. Tightwad's work over the years. At our house these days, my wife and I are grappling with a lot of familiar issues, such as: "How much allowance is enough?" "What things should the kids buy with their own money, what with ours?" "How can kids learn to contribute to charity?" and "What should we tell them about our family's finances?" The challenge is to solicit their ideas, steer them in wise directions, and never sound preachy.

More than once I've caught myself on the verge of blurting out, "When I was your age . . ." I try to nip the impulse in the bud, before that veil of boredom descends on my kids' glazed-over eyeballs. I know too well the pitfalls of trying to teach kids by historical allusion, even lively stories drawn from one's own childhood. The first pitfall is relevance. Our kids are living in today's world, and while there are certain eternal constants, there are also many circumstances today that are vastly different from our childhoods.

The second pitfall is the adult's tendency toward faulty memory—or at best selective recall. How many of us can accurately remember the amount of our allowance when we were 10? Or what certain toys and items of clothing cost, or what our parents bought for us, or whether Johnny down the street did or didn't have a TV in his room when he was 12?

Faulty memory is compounded by the problem of translating yesteryear's *nominally* lower consumer prices to today's *seemingly* higher prices. If we don't adjust those prices for the enormous inflation of the last three decades, we will be kidding ourselves—and our children—into thinking that the *real* price of everything has gone up.

In fact, relative to typical earnings then and now, the prices of countless goods and services—ranging from food and televisions to toys and airline tickets—have *declined* in real terms. The candy bar of your youth may have cost only a nickel or dime (and perhaps was bigger, too), but your allowance was similarly modest, and so perhaps was your father's salary. So the next time you catch yourself about to launch into the "When I was young" sermon to your kids, remember to put your mental price inflator on all the numbers you're about to summon up.

To give you a little help, I consulted a handy table of the U.S. Consumer Price Index going back several decades. For any prices you're recalling from the 1950s, you should multiply them by about five to figure out how much they would be today if they had simply matched the general rate of inflation. The multiplier for 1965 prices would be about the same, five; 1975 prices should be multiplied by three; 1985, by about 1.5.

If today's price for the same or similar product is lower than that adjusted amount, then the item is actually less expensive today than when you were young, regardless of the nominally higher price. And even if today's price really is higher after adjusting for inflation—which is the case, for example, for most full-size automobiles—remember that some of that higher price is probably the result of improvements in quality, features and durability.

So when you're talking to your kids about "the good ol' days" or the "tough times of my childhood" (depending on what point you're trying to make),

keep your frames of reference clear. Be a good economic educator while you're making your point. But
don't be surprised if your kids *still* find the whole lesson pretty irrelevant to their lives today.

This book is a companion to Kiplinger's *Money-
Smart Kids (And Parents, Too!),* a more-extensive reference in which Janet Bodnar covers additional financial issues of interest to parents and their children. It
contains more information on the topics in this
book, plus many not covered here, including how to
use insurance and wills to protect your family's
future, how to save and pay for college, even how to
make your child a millionaire (in much-inflated
future dollars!) through savvy investing. To order a
copy, call 800–727–7015.

Used together or separately, both books are
guaranteed to help parents build not only the value
of their family's financial assets, but also a family tradition of financial values. Your kids will grow up with
a healthy attitude toward money and the ability to
manage it, so they will become fulfilled, competent
adults (and won't land back on your doorstep after
you thought the nest was empty).

From all of us in the Kiplinger organization,
our best wishes for success in raising truly Money-
Smart Kids.

*Knight Kiplinger*

# Why You Need A Snappy Comeback

**W**hen it comes to money, kids ask the darnedest questions. Parents on the receiving end find their children's queries:

- **Exasperating:** "Mom, can I have that?"

- **Amusing:** "How much will I get from the tooth fairy?"

- **Puzzling:** "Why is a nickel bigger than a dime?"

- **Awkward:** "How much money do you make?"

- **Embarrassing:** "How come you two are always fighting about money?"

It's from family discussions about subjects like these that children will learn their most lasting lessons about the value—and the values—of money. You can't count on kids learning much about money management in school, and you don't want them learning from the media or from their friends. That leaves things squarely up to you.

Unfortunately, kids and their questions can't be scripted. On the contrary, you can count on them catching you off guard, when you're least prepared to answer. Ill at ease or in a hurry, we've all given our kids the bum's rush at one time or another, with an abbreviated, even abrupt, response—usually along the lines of "Yes," "No," or "Maybe."

## Yes, No, Maybe

In the "yes" group are parents who take the path of least resistance—or maybe they just like to spend money. "Since she's been born, I've hardly bought myself anything. I'd rather spend on her," one parent told *Forbes* magazine in an article titled "Babies As Dolls," about the booming market for infant clothing and equipment. Said another parent, "My kids have tons of stuff, but if they want something I just don't know how to say no." And these kids are barely old enough to ask a question. Imagine the scene when they really turn up the heat at age 8 or 13—or 21 or 35.

At the other extreme are parents who respond with a knee-jerk "no" that's commendable but ineffective. Their strong stand is undermined by a shaky foundation because they don't bother to explain why they're denying whatever it is their kids want.

In the vast middle—and we've all been there—are the wafflers, who, when put on the spot, respond with a resounding "maybe" in any of its forms: "We'll see." "I don't know." "Go ask your mother/father." "Do you think I'm made of money?" For lack of a great comeback, we take refuge in the flip response, the old cliché, the evasive answer—anything to avoid the question. And we miss a golden opportunity to teach a mini-lesson in money values. Besides, kids are people, too, and they deserve to have their questions taken seriously and answered thoughtfully.

# A Handy Guide

This book is your source for a snappy comeback, a handy guide to answering even your kids' most sensitive questions about money. It's filled with responses that will get you out of a jam, fill a void, smooth over an awkward moment, satisfy your children's curiosity and leave them with something to think about so they're less likely to bring up the subject again.

In these pages, you'll find more than 100 of the queries that are asked most frequently by kids between preschool and high school, from around ages 5 to 16. As a jumping-off point for discussion, we've included typical responses by parents that miss the mark—as well as others that are models of quick thinking. Then as Dr. T, I'll chime in with a prescription for how you should handle the situation the next time around.

Scattered throughout this book you'll also find boxes labeled "Prices Then & Now." In them we compare the cost of things you may have bought—or your family may have owned—when you were a kid with an equivalent item today. The boxes are an entertaining reminder of life in the "good old days," but they have a serious purpose as well. Your frame of reference can be a source of friction between you and your children. Your memories are different from their realities—and your memories may not be as accurate as you think. Using the information in the boxes, you can actually construct a market basket of things children buy to see how a kid's cost of living has changed over the years.

Back in the 1960s, for example, a kid could have watched a movie and eaten a bag of M&M's for less than a dollar. Today the same treat would cost more than $4.50—an increase of over 400%. If you think your kids should be paying for their own movie tickets and treats, remember that number when you set their allowance. Even though inflation alone would have brought the price to over $5, $4.50 is still a lot for your kid to shell out. If you could afford to buy something in 1965 but your kids can't afford to buy it today, they're probably being underpaid.

On the other hand, children and families today also have possessions you never dreamed of—video games and computers spring immediately to mind. The standard family car costs more, but comes equipped with air conditioning, air bags—and cup holders. In your youth the family probably shared listening time on one large stereo that sat in the living room. Today, each of your children might have a portable CD player in his or her bedroom.

Changing times and increasing affluence are challenges for parents, who have to grapple with how much of this stuff they want to buy—and how much of the consumer culture they want to buy into. Dr. T doesn't pretend to have all the answers. The advice dispensed here can't create more money in households where there's simply not enough. The prescribed strategies won't work unless parents are willing to talk with each other and with their children. And some problems are beyond the scope of this book. If you suspect that a child is using his allowance to buy drugs, for example, how much of an allowance to give is the least of your worries. Cut off all funds and get professional help.

Overall, Dr. T's aim is to offer reasonable solutions in a readable form that real people will find useful—and even entertaining.

# Mom, Can I Have That?

**I**t starts with a cookie in the supermarket when the children are still small enough to ride in the grocery cart, reaches a peak when they're 16 and want wheels of their own, and includes hundreds of variations during the years in between. In fact, it sometimes seems as if "Can I have that?" is the *only* question kids ask about money.

You might expect that Dr. T would advise just saying no, and most times that's not a bad idea. But your kids will be more inclined to take no for an answer if it's followed by a reason. A simple "because I said so" is sometimes acceptable, but if you don't offer more of a rationale than that kids will be tempted to chip away at your resolve in hopes of changing your mind.

Of course, many times you're going to say yes. Part of the fun of being a parent is buying things for your children or taking them places you enjoy, too. But if you say yes you should do it because you want to—not because you're desperate to get out of a store or afraid to stand up to your children.

# "Can I have a cookie?"

(Your 4-year-old in the grocery cart seat)

## You're tempted to say:

"Sure." (It's a small price to pay to head off a temper tantrum.)

## Dr. T's Rx:

Give in *that* easily and in the next aisle your child will want a sweet cereal, in the next aisle a candy bar, in the next aisle a soft drink, in the next aisle a frozen yogurt.

| Prices Then & Now | | |
|---|---|---|
| 1970 | chewing gum (5-stick pack) | 5¢ |
| 1980 | chewing gum (7-stick pack) | 20¢ |
| Present | chewing gum (5-stick pack) | 25¢ |

*To adjust earlier prices to account for the effects of inflation, multiply 1970 price by 4 and 1980 price by 1.75.*

*Prices courtesy of Wm. Wrigley Jr. Company*

Next time, try leaving your 4-year-old at home. Failing that, lay down the rules in advance. Tell your kids they may each choose one treat—either a cookie OR a candy bar OR a box of sweet cereal OR whatever else is appropriate. If they settle on the first thing they see, remind them that they get only one choice and they might want to think about other possibilities before making a final decision. That should keep your kids busy and get you off the hook. They'll be so eager to see what new goodies are waiting around the next corner that, with luck, you can hold off buying anything until your shopping trip is just about over.

It isn't saying no that brings on a temper tantrum. It's saying no after a string of yeses that tempts your kids to test your sincerity with a stream of tears. They'll soon tire of the tactic if they know the rules ahead of time and are convinced you'll stick to them. Setting limits early and often heads off even bigger confrontations later (see the following questions).

# "Can I have a new G.I Joe?"

(Your 8-year-old in the toy store while you shop for another child's birthday gift)

### You're tempted to say:

"Sure." (It's still a small price to pay to avoid a temper tantrum.)

### Dr. T's Rx:

See the preceding answer, but with a twist. At this age, you have another option in addition to leaving your kids at home or granting them one request. By the time they're 8 years old, they probably have financial resources of their own. Tell them you're going to the toy store to buy someone else a gift, and if they want something for themselves they'll have to bring their own money.

12-18

**"Would you like to hear the top
ten list of things I want this year?"**

*Reprinted with special permission of King Features Syndicate*

*If it's your wallet you're worried about, there's no better way to teach kids the value of a buck than to make them ante up their own.*

# "Can I have those $150 sneakers?"

(Your 12-year-old in a shoe store)

### You're tempted to say:

"Not on your life!"

### Dr. T's Rx:

Prepare for the Big Scene you've prided yourself on avoiding for the last eight years. If your kids have been hearing "sure" since they were four, they're not going to accept one "not on your life" without a fight.

On the other hand, if you've been following the advice in the preceding questions your children may not even bother to ask for those expensive sneakers. You can guarantee that by discussing with your kids *before* you go shopping how much you're willing to pay for shoes, so that you're not put on the spot in the store. Kids this age are old enough to know that buying their shoes is only one of many demands on your income. They also have access to more cash than they did when they were younger and can appreciate the art of dealmaking. Tell them that your budget allows $50 (or whatever) for sneakers, so they can either shop for a pair that fits the price or pay the extra out of their own pockets.

If you object in principle to paying more than $50 (or whatever) for sneakers, then just say no. But if it's your wallet you're worried about, there's no better way to teach kids the value of a buck than to make them ante up their own. With a vested interest in what they buy, they're more likely to appreciate and take care of it. Nudge them toward discount stores or sales, and they'll get a lesson in smart shopping.

This doesn't count as indulging your child. Dr. T suspects that if kids have to come up with $50 or more for a pair of shoes that will be outgrown or out of style in six months, they'll think twice about buying a second pair.

## "Can I have that Batman lunch box?"

(Asked when you're shopping for school supplies)

### You're tempted to say:

"Sure." (Anything to get out of here quicker.)

### Dr. T's Rx:

This is one of those times you can give in without guilt. You have to buy a lunch box anyway and it's a relatively inexpensive item, so you might as well let your kids make the choice. And the next time they accuse you of never buying them anything they want, you can always come back with, "Sure I do. Remember the Batman lunch box?"

## "Can I have [fill in the blank]?"

(Asked by *any* child of *any* age about *anything* when all you want to do is get through your list and get out of the store)

### You're tempted to say:

"We'll see." (Anything to get out of here quicker.)

### Dr. T's Rx:

No matter how frazzled you are, "No" is *always* preferable to "We'll see." If your children detect any wavering at all, they will immediately assume it means yes. Tell your kids you are buying what's on your list and *only* what's on your list. If there's any reason at all why you shouldn't deny their request outright— maybe they've asked for a new folder for school or something similarly noble that they know you're a sucker for—at least be specific in telling them that "School supplies are for another trip," by which time their urge to buy may have passed.

*No matter how frazzled you are, "No" is always preferable to "We'll see."*

# "I saw the neatest game on TV today. Can I have it?"

### *You're tempted to say:*
"I'm going to get rid of that TV."

### *Dr. T's Rx:*

Don't fall back on threats you have no intention of making good on. In this case, a simple no will do.

You're actually dealing with two issues here. One is the steady stream of TV-inspired requests, but that's probably the lesser of your problems. Younger children especially have short memories. What they ask for today they likely will have forgotten about tomorrow, as long as you don't go out and buy it for them.

The bigger issue isn't so much the stuff as the *commercials* that push the stuff. Kids are prime targets for the hype—and the hyperactivity—of today's TV ads. They're also primed for a letdown when the toys inevitably turn out to be less than they appear.

There's something to be said for being mugged by reality, but you can soften the blow by sitting down with your children and watching what they watch so you can explain what's going on. Young children, for example, don't always know where the show ends and the commercial begins. They don't understand, unless you tell them, that all those lights and visual effects, all that noise and color, are intended to sell them something that may not measure up to their expectations. Older children can get into sophisticated discussions about why famous sports stars or actresses would pitch a particular brand of shoes or soft drinks or jeans. Do they *really* wear that stuff—

## Small Change
• • • • • • • • • • • • • • • • • • • • • • • •

According to federal law, any reproduction of U.S. currency must be at *least* 1½ times larger than the original, *or* no larger than ¾ of the actual size. No matter what the size, you can never reproduce pictures of currency in color!

or are they just being paid to say they do?

And kids are fascinated by the tricks of the TV trade. (Did you know, for example, that on-camera chocolate bars and dollops of ketchup are really molds made of resin, a substance used to make plastics?) Each year the readers of *Zillions,* the consumer magazine for children, hand out ZAP awards ("ZAP it off the air, please") to commercials and products that didn't live up to their billing.

Studies show that simply talking to your kids about ads can make a difference in how they regard commercials and how much they ask for. Once children understand what's going on, they'll be less likely to bug you, and that's a guarantee from Dr. T.

"No, he can't really fly...no, the bad guys don't really have a ray gun...no, this cereal really isn't the best food in the whole world...no, it won't make you strong as a giant..."

*Harris/Cartoonists & Writers Syndicate*

*Sometimes just writing down all the things they'd like to have is satisfaction enough for kids.*

# "Dad, can I put just one more thing on my Christmas list?"

## You're tempted to say:
"If you do, Santa will think you're greedy and won't bring you *anything.*"

## Dr. T's Rx:
Putting something on a list isn't necessarily greedy. Expecting to get everything you ask for *is* greedy. Both parents and children should learn the difference.

Let your kids make their holiday lists as lengthy as they want, as long as they understand that what they're making is a wish list from which Santa, Mom and Dad, and other gift-givers can choose items.

Remind your kids that whittling down their list to a reasonable length can pay off. With all the work Santa has to do around the holidays, he probably won't have time to read much more than, say, 10 or 12 items. And the shorter the list, the more likely that Santa will remember what's on it.

One of the best bits of modern-day wisdom Dr. T ever heard on this point came from a great shopping mall Santa who didn't bat an eyelash when one youngster handed him a list of 28 toys. Santa patiently reviewed the list and told the child he'd plug it into his computer to see what came up as available. What he actually brought, said Santa, would depend on how much room he had in his sleigh.

Holiday wish lists are for parents as well as kids, and can work to your advantage in a number of ways:

- **Lists are an outlet for some of the holiday "buy-me-that" pressure.** Sometimes just writing down all the things they'd like to have is satisfaction enough for kids. A toy that a child really, really wants in October may be totally forgotten by December. In Dr. T's personal experience, children frequently make—and misplace—a number of different lists before settling on the one that goes to Santa.

- **Lists give you an opportunity to teach your kids how to set priorities.** Take those lengthy lists your children have been constructing and have them rank the top ten items. Holiday catalogs can be a big help with older kids, who can appreciate how much everything costs. Ask the children what they'd keep on their list if they had, say, $200 to spend. (Remember, though, that this is just an exercise!)

- **Lists are an organizing tool for your own holiday shopping.** After all, you and other family members are going to be buying gifts for the kiddies anyway. You'll be less frazzled and more focused, and get your shopping done more quickly, if you know what you're looking for.

At some point, of course, it's up to you to set a limit on how much stuff you buy. Dr. T offers a few guidelines on when to call a halt:

## You Know You've Gone Overboard When...

- You're embarrassed to tell your friends how many presents you bought for your kids.

- You can't find enough hiding places for all the gifts.

- You can't remember what you hid.

- In their zeal to open all the gifts, your kids resemble sharks on a feeding frenzy.

- In the middle of opening gifts, your kids get bored and walk away.

It's tough to put a number on just what that point is, since every family has its own gift-giving tradition. Three gifts may be two too many for a toddler who can't appreciate them, or for an older child who's getting a new computer. But three gifts is probably too few if you like to surprise your family with inexpensive stocking-stuffers.

*Take those lengthy lists your children have been constructing and have them rank the top ten items.*

*Wrap everything in sight, on the theory that to a kid, all gift-wrapped boxes are treasures.*

If you need a number as a guideline, consider that families annually spend around $325 per child on toys, and a majority of them are bought during the holidays, according to the Toy Manufacturers Association, an industry group. Dr. T recommends starting with a nice round ten presents—three "big" ones and seven "smaller gifts"—and adjusting up or down depending on how much you want to spend.

Included in that total should be things you would have had to buy your children anyway, such as gloves, earmuffs or a new backpack to replace the one with the broken strap. Wrap everything in sight, on the theory that to a kid, *all* gift-wrapped boxes are treasures. The boxes don't have to be physically large, and the gifts inside don't have to be expensive. But opening them prolongs the kids' pleasure without increasing your expense. When her children were younger Dr. T even wrapped each Golden Book individually, although the kids eventually caught on to that gambit.

One of the best gifts you can give your kids is time—presenting them with a certificate entitling them to an afternoon or evening of your undivided attention for an activity of their choosing.

In the end, the real test of a successful holiday isn't the number of gifts you buy or how much they cost, but how well-suited they are to your children and how well they wear. It's only natural for kids to play with the glamour gifts first—Nerf weapons, American Girls dolls, anything electronic. But if, on December 26, they ask you to try the new board game, and on February 13 they build the model rocket, and on July 23 they start the third book in the complete Anne of Green Gables series, then you'll know you didn't go overboard.

# "Can I have one of those big Barbie convertibles [or Batmobiles] that runs on batteries so I can sit behind the wheel and drive?"

### You're tempted to say:
"No."

### Dr. T's Rx:

Stick with no. But you can always improve on a negative response by telling your children why you're denying their request. If you think self-propelled vehicles are too dangerous, too expensive, or just plain too grown-up for kids who should be getting around via pedal power, say so. Your kids will know you've given your response some serious thought and aren't just trying to put them off—and they won't be disappointed when they don't find a convertible under the tree.

Fiddy/Cartoonists & Writers Syndicate

# "If you won't buy it for me [or can't find it in the stores], why can't I ask Santa for it?"

### You're tempted to say:

(Face it. They've stumped you.)

### Dr. T's Rx:

It's time to give your kids the lowdown on Santa: Santa's elves don't really make all those toys. Sure, they can handle trains, building blocks, and stuffed animals. But when it comes to sophisticated

## Child's Play

Talking with your children about money needn't be a chore. On the contrary, it can be child's play—literally. Even in today's high-tech world, some of the best teaching tools available to parents are low-tech board games. Here's a selection of classics and promising newcomers, all kid-tested by Dr. T's panel of experts.

**The Game of Life** (Milton Bradley, $15). A big hit among children of all ages because "it covers everything," in the words of one 11-year-old. "Everything" includes careers, college loans, mortgages, car insurance, dividends and taxes—an entire money-management course. Younger children may need some help reading the words, but they don't seem to have much trouble grasping the concepts.

**Payday** (Parker Brothers, $15). A close second because "it's fun and funny." (One card reads, "Pay Tick Tock, Inc. We cleaned your clock.") The idea is to get from one payday to the next with money to spare. Kids love to take a chance when they land on the lottery square, but it's gratifying to hear them groan when they're instructed to pick up bills from the mailbox or pay a "monster charge"—with interest.

**The Allowance Game** (Lakeshore Learning Materials; 800–421–5354, $14.95 plus $3.50 shipping and handling). Ranks up there with Payday because it's easy for younger children to understand and appreciate. As they make a circuit of the board, players are instructed to do things "that kids really do," such as play a video game or forget their homework. And the money denominations are manageable: The first player to save $20 is the winner.

**Monopoly** (Parker Brothers, $12). Still popular, although from a child's standpoint this game's slower pace and longer playing time (does it *ever* end?) is a drawback. And compared with the other electronic gizmos like robots and video games, Santa often has to get them from the manufacturer.

If an elf-made toy is a blockbuster, the elves may not be able to keep up with demand. Or if they have to rely on the factory to supply the season's biggest hit, they may be subject to shortages just like everyone else.

Santa gets a volume discount, of course, and sometimes manufacturers are willing to give him toys because it's good advertising. But there are limits to a list as long as his, so children can't expect to get every toy they ask for.

And if mom and dad think a toy is too expensive or otherwise unsuitable, Santa won't do an end run around them and put his job in jeopardy.

games, "you only do one thing," says a 10-year-old—buy and sell property. Parents can pick up the pace, and pique the interest of younger kids by making a slight change in the rules: Let players start building houses and hotels as soon as all the properties are purchased, even if they don't own a monopoly.

**Monopoly Junior** (Parker Brothers, $10). A welcome alternative to the senior version for both children and adults because you can actually finish a game in a reasonable amount of time. Instead of Boardwalk and Park Place, players buy Bumper Cars, Roller Coaster and other attractions at an amusement park, and charge each other admission instead of rent. The money denominations are smaller than in regular Monopoly, and the playing pieces are bigger—no little green houses to keep track of.

**Presto Change-O** (Educational Insights; 800–933–3277, $24.95). At first blush the idea seems too simple: Follow the "Earn" and "Spend" directions on a circuit of the board and be the first to save $10. But there's a trick: Your stock of cash can never include more than one nickel, two dimes, three quarters, four $1 bills or one $5 bill, so, presto change-o, you're constantly rebalancing your accounts to make the right change. A 7-year-old found it "challenging"—and so did his mother.

**Careers** (Parker Brothers). This classic isn't on the market right now, but look for it at yard sales (Dr. T's kids rescued an old but intact set from a neighbor's trash pile). Players choose their "success formula"—a combination of money, fame and happiness—and enter various occupations trying to collect the right number of dollars, stars and hearts. The game took a while to finish, but the kids enjoyed it enough to play again. "A little like Life," they concluded. Hint: Fame can be easier to achieve than fortune.

# "Why won't you buy me a new video-game system? All the other kids have one."

### You're tempted to say:

"If all the *other* kids jumped off the Empire State Building, would you jump, too?"

### Dr. T's Rx:

Don't try to be too clever or you'll end up outsmarting yourself. Kids won't necessarily make the connection between jumping off buildings and buying video games (or if they do, they'll probably ignore it).

Say what you mean, which, Dr. T hopes, is that "because everyone has it" is the *last* reason you'd consider buying something. It's critical that your children understand that your family's values may not be the same as the Jones family's. Maybe you can't afford to keep up. Maybe you feel your children's current video-game system is in good enough shape and they don't need a new one (unless you're willing to let them buy it with their own money). Or maybe you just don't want to referee disputes between siblings about whose turn it is to play (in which case you might consider compromising on a couple of hand-held game systems).

## Money Talks

• • • • • • • • • • • • • • • • • • • • •

Even though we don't officially have a "penny" (we use the cent), we've got lots of penny-based expressions in our language. Most of them could probably be traced back to English phrases. Here are just a few:

- **Penny**-wise, pound foolish
- A **penny** for your thoughts
- In for a **penny,** in for a pound
- **Penny** pincher
- A pretty **penny**
- A **penny** saved is a **penny** earned

We've also got expressions based on "dollar," such as:

- Bet your bottom **dollar**
- (Bet you) **dollars** to doughnuts
- Sound as a **dollar**
- **Dollar** diplomacy

In any case, the decision is up to you, not the Joneses. And whatever you decide, your kids will not be social outcasts, they will not die (*you* didn't when *you* tried the same ploy), and they will not stop loving you or move out of the house.

That doesn't mean you should never buy your kids *anything* all the other kids have. It just means you shouldn't buy them *everything* all the other kids have. Be discriminating, choosing those things your kids want most—and, if you've done your job, least expect. The element of surprise is more than half the fun for both of you.

A single mother on a limited budget tells the story of her young daughter, who wanted the same expensive doll that all her friends were playing with. Mother and daughter talked it over and started a savings fund. But when Mom saw her daughter cutting out pictures of the coveted doll and pasting them on her old doll's face, she broke down and bought her daughter the doll as an Easter gift—only to fret that she had given in too easily.

She needn't have worried. The child did get her doll early, but not before her mother had talked with her about their limited means and the need to save for purchases—a lesson that wasn't lost on the little girl. "There must be an Easter Bunny," she told her mom, "because *you* never could have afforded this."

*Reprinted by permission: Tribune Media Services*

# "Look, we can get ten free hours of computer time! Can we sign up?"

### You're tempted to say:

"I'm glad to see you're taking an interest in computers instead of video games."

### Dr. T's Rx:

You may not be so glad once you get the bill after those ten free hours are up. For years parents have battled chatty kids over big phone bills, but you haven't seen anything till you've seen online charges rung up by kids hooked on chat rooms, the super-party lines of the '90s. "My daughter's bill was over $50 the first month," says one mom. "Then my son got absorbed in an interactive video game and his bill was nearly $80."

Make the most of your children's interest in the information superhighway, but set some rules of the road and make them pay their own tolls. Tell the kids

| Prices Then & Now | M&M's | Milky Way | Snickers |
|---|---|---|---|
| 1960 | 5¢ (28.4grams) | 5¢ (44.5 grams) | 5¢ (43.9 grams) |
| 1970 | 10¢ (40.5 grams) | 10¢ (55.3 grams) | 10¢ (51.9 grams) |
| 1980 | 25¢ (43.0 grams) | 25¢ (58.0 grams) | 25¢ (55.0 grams) |
| Present | 40¢ (48.1 grams) | 40¢ (60.8 grams) | 40¢ (58.7 grams) |

*To adjust earlier prices to account for the effects of inflation, multiply 1960 prices by 5, 1970 prices by 4 and 1980 prices by 1.75.*

*Prices and weights courtesy of Mars, Inc.*

you'll pay the basic charge—usually around $10 a month for five hours—but after that's used up they're on their own time. Sign up with a service that uses individual screen names or numbers for each user, so you can easily tell who has been on for how long by looking at the bill or monitoring charges during the month with the online billing features.

Other ways to keep costs in check:

- **Keep the computer in an open location,** such as a family room or den, instead of a child's own room. It's easier to keep track of how much time the kids are online, and what they're doing there.

- **Take advantage of "parental control" options**. Online services offer these as a way for parents to limit access to areas that aren't suitable for kids, but you can also use them to keep children out of areas where they can rack up big bills.

- **Look for cheaper alternatives.** An online service will charge you a basic rate, plus an extra fee (around $3) for each additional hour. But if all you want to do is send e-mail or connect to the Internet, you may get a better deal by bypassing online services and hooking up directly to the 'Net for a flat fee of around $20 per month or even less.

- **Get free computer time.** Freelancers hired by online services to host chat rooms or monitor bulletin boards are often compensated with free online time. So are some experts—teachers, for example, who volunteer to go online to help kids with their homework. Check out the possibilities with the service that's running the room or forum you're interested in.

- **Pull the plug** if you think the money or the time is getting out hand. In the family cited earlier in this question, Mom made her daughter pay the $50 and then canceled the service. "It's a solitary activity that pulls kids out of the family," she says. After her son paid his $80 bill, he canceled the service himself.

*If yours is the type of child who shows initial enthusiasm but quickly becomes bored, don't feel obliged to gratify his latest fancy.*

# "Can I play ice hockey?"

(Or gymnastics, swimming, or any other sport that can't be played in your backyard and requires more than a ball and a pair of sneakers)

## You're tempted to say:

"Why can't you just stick to basketball?"

## Dr. T's Rx:

Put your kids' latest request in context with all the other things they do. Financial considerations aside, there's no reason to add yet another activity if their schedule is already fully booked. Dr. T recommends a "rule of three": No more than three days a week per child of activities that require being chauffeured (so soccer practice twice a week counts as two, but piano lessons at school don't count). If there's no room in your kids' schedule for anything else, expensive or otherwise, the answer to their request should be obvious.

Likewise, if yours is the type of child who shows initial enthusiasm but quickly becomes bored, don't feel obliged to gratify his latest fancy. Tell him you'll have to see some sustained interest in street hockey before you're willing to shell out several hundred dollars for ice hockey equipment and rink time.

But suppose yours is a serious child whose request isn't out of the question—just expensive. Test her commitment by telling her she'll have to make choices: If she wants to swim two or three times a week, she'll have to give up gymnastics. If he really wants to try ice hockey, he'll start with used equipment. Once you launch your kids into an activity, they can contribute to extras, or you might hold these out as a reward: For every 15 minutes of practice, let's say, your budding tennis star earns credits toward a new racquet. Once they reach a certain number of credits, you'll spring for the coveted piece of equipment, or at least split the cost.

# "If I don't spend all my lunch money, can I keep it and use it for something else?"

### You're tempted to say:

"As long as you take your lunch to school."

### Dr. T's Rx:

That may sound like a reasonable deal, but think about what you're getting yourself into. If your child habitually avoids the cafeteria, she doesn't need lunch money, which becomes a de facto raise in her allowance. If you think a raise is in order, give her one. If not, stop shelling out money for phantom lunches and keep packing those bologna sandwiches.

Lunch money appears to be a hot button among many parents. Here's a sampling of the mail Dr. T received in response to a column about older children paying for their own school lunches:

"I disagree that children should pay for their school lunches with their own allowance. Snacks, concert tickets and special 'trendy' clothing can certainly be financed through the allowance or the child's financial assets. But food, clothing and shelter are typical categories that are the traditional responsibility of parents."

"In your recent column you included lunch money in a child's allowance. This should never happen. I have too often seen middle and high school youngsters skipping lunch or just buying a snack in order to save money for other things they wanted."

"As a parent it is my duty to provide lunch. There is always lunch money in the designated drawer if my children decide they do not wish to pack their own lunch. They are expected to return any change to the drawer if they eat light. The kids do what they wish (within reason) with their allowance, but the lunch money does not belong to them."

By suggesting that older children could be responsible for their lunches, Dr. T assumes that parents would provide this money over and above the kids' discretionary income, and that the kids' main responsibility would be to manage it.

However, if you suspect that your kids aren't up to the challenge or would starve themselves to buy a new pair of jeans, rethink your strategy: Dole out lunch money one day at a time, require kids to return any unspent cash, or bag the lunch money—and bag the lunch.

## "Why do we have to buy my clothes at The Bargain Barrel? Why can't we shop at Chez Chic, where the other kids go?"

### You're tempted to say:

"If The Bargain Barrel is good enough for me, it's good enough for you."

### Dr. T's Rx:

As a regular customer of The Bargain Barrel, Dr. T's on your side. But you're more likely to make your point if you're willing to compromise. Make a deal with your kids. If your conscience and your wallet allow, tell them you'll buy an item or two from this season's "name" store, but not their whole wardrobe. So your son might choose the baggy shirt all the kids are wearing, but wear it over standard-issue jeans. With a limited amount to spend at the store of choice, he'll be inspired to shop harder for bargains or clearance sales (guided by you, of course).

Now you've turned a classic confrontation into a win-win situation: Your kids learn how to look cool on a budget, and you still have your pocketbook and your principles intact.

# Are We Rich or Poor?

**A**t some point in their lives, and it will come sooner than you think, your children will reach the age of reason: They'll notice that other kids have things they don't have, and they'll want to know why. They'll pose questions that you'll find particularly sensitive because they cut right to the heart of your family's finances—how much you make and how that stacks up against other families. Parents have a tendency to deflect this kind of question as too hot to handle.

But it's easier than you think to give your kids answers that will satisfy them if you keep two things in mind: First, you don't have to tell them everything. They're not looking for an accounting of every dollar sign and decimal point. What they really want is a general idea of how you're doing (and whether now is a good time to ask you for the new bike they have their eye on).

Second, you're more self-conscious about the subject than they are. Like questions about sex, kids usually pose questions about money out of innocent curiosity and youthful naivete. If you don't raise an eyebrow, neither will they.

# "How much money do you make?"

### You're tempted to say:
"That's none of your business."

### Dr. T's Rx:

Instead of dismissing the question so abruptly, it's better to go with an answer that's vague but more polite, as in "More than some families but not as much as others." That's a nicer way of not answering the question, which you shouldn't feel obliged to do. When it comes to teaching kids about money, parents have lots of responsibilities. Telling your kids how much you make isn't necessarily one of them.

| Prices Then & Now | | |
|---|---|---|
| 1965 | Ford Galaxie (family car) | $ 2,678 |
| 1975 | Ford Granada (family car) | $ 3,756 |
| Present | Ford Taurus (family car) | $19,150 |

*To adjust earlier prices to account for the effects of inflation, multiply 1965 price by 5 and the 1975 price by 3. Note that inflation is not the only contributing factor in the rise of car prices. Among other things, cars have become safer and more fuel-efficient and comfortable, and these features add cost—and value—to the car's price.*

*Prices taken from the Automobile Manufacturers Association and Chrome Data's PC Carbook.*

For one thing, no matter how much you make, whether it's $30,000 or $130,000, grade school kids (and even high-schoolers) will have trouble putting it in perspective. It will sound like an enormous sum to your children—certainly more than enough to buy the $100 bicycle or $200 video game system they want. For another thing, you have a right to your privacy. While it's certainly desirable to talk with your kids about money (that is, after all, what this book is all about) you can't be blamed for not wanting your affairs blabbed around the neighborhood— which your kids will almost certainly do, if only in innocent conversation.

Besides, when young children ask this question chances are they don't care about the numbers anyway. They're just trying to get an idea of your relative wealth and where you stand vis-a-vis other families.

They'd also be relieved if you assured them that you're not at risk of being turned out into the street.

As your kids get older you may choose to be more forthright about how much you earn. But it will make more sense to your children, and be more comfortable for you, if you put your income in the context of your expenses. Kids need to know, for example, that after taxes your take-home pay is a lot less than your actual salary. They need to know that you can't spend money on just anything because you have to cover certain fixed expenses first, such as the mortgage and the car insurance. One dad gave his teens a crash course in household finances by converting his pay into dollar bills, stacking the money on the table and inviting his kids to watch the pile dwindle as he paid the monthly bills.

Some parents have even turned over the bill-paying chores to their kids. "For several years, since Mary was 12, I have given her the bills and the checkbook and she does the rest," one mother wrote to Dr. T. "I just do a quick review and sign the checks." What many adults would find tedious Mary finds fascinating, says her mom. "From this experience she not only acquires the skill of managing a checkbook, but also gains a real sense of what it costs to run a household on a month-by-month basis."

*It will make more sense to your children, and be more comfortable for you, if you put your income in the context of your expenses.*

*Calvin and Hobbes © 1995 Watterson. Dist. by Universal Press Syndicate. Reprinted with permission. All rights reserved.*

*Explain that watching where your money goes doesn't mean you're poor. It just means you have to parcel out your income to cover lots of different expenses.*

# "Are we poor?"

(Often preceded by "You never buy me *anything.*")

### You're tempted to say:

"We *would* be if I bought you everything you asked for."

### Dr. T's Rx:

Typical middle-class families aren't poor (even though it sometimes feels that way), and it would be misleading and unfair to let your kids think you are, even unintentionally.

But your funds are limited, and kids don't understand the concept of limits, especially as it applies to them. Explain that watching where your money goes doesn't mean you're poor. It just means you have to parcel out your income to cover lots of different expenses (for suggestions on creative ways of saying no to specific purchases, see Chapter 2).

A variation of this question is, "Why are you so cheap?" Assuming that your child is being serious and not merely fresh, explain that shopping for the best price or deciding not to buy something doesn't mean you're cheap, just that you want to make your money go as far as it can.

It might help to give your kids more hands-on experience in the art of managing money. The next time you buy the kids' back-to-school clothes, for example, tell them in advance how much you can afford to spend and then let them have a hand in choosing the wardrobe without busting the budget.

If your children must have a misconception about your financial status, it's healthier for them to think you're poor and cheap rather than rich and extravagant!

# "Are we rich?"

## You're tempted to say:
"Whatever gave you that idea?"

## Dr. T's Rx:
Your lifestyle may have given them that idea. Even if you don't feel rich, you probably live comfortably enough that your kids think you are. Or maybe their curiosity was piqued by a specific event—you bought a new car, for example, remodeled your house or got a job promotion.

In any event, answering the question with one of your own isn't such a bad idea. It gives you a chance to find out what's on your child's mind, and gives you a few seconds to get your thoughts together. "Are we rich?" is similar to "How much do you make?" in that it demands a diplomatic answer that will still satisfy the children. One mom didn't miss a beat when her 6-year-old put her on the spot. "We're not rich," she replied, "but we have enough money to buy the things we need and some left over to share."

Now, if your name happens to be Rockefeller, you'll eventually have to tell your kids that you are, in fact, rich. But the rest of the advice in this book should be as helpful to you as to any other parent.

---

## Small Change
● ● ● ● ● ● ● ● ● ● ● ● ● ● ● ● ● ● ● ● ● ●

In 1861, President Lincoln's Secretary of the Treasury decreed that banknotes should be printed with green ink on the back (hence "greenbacks.") During the Civil War, the Confederate States printed their own money, called "graybacks" or "bluebacks."

# "How come we don't have a big-screen TV like the Joneses?"

### You're tempted to say:

"If you don't like it here, why don't you move in with the Joneses?"

### Dr. T's Rx:

Unless you really expect your kids to move in with the Joneses (and a big-screen TV can be very tempting), stick to answering the question, whatever the answer may be: "Because we can't afford a big-screen TV," or "Because we're saving our money for a trip to Disney World next spring," or "Because we think a big-screen TV is a waste of money." Kids are willing to accept the truth when it's offered. If you're on a tight budget, say so. With luck, your kids won't bug you for other stuff. If you can afford something but choose not to buy it, say so. Your kids will get a lesson in family values.

Sometimes a question like this is just an attempt by your kids to make you feel guilty. But sometimes kids are genuinely curious about where you fit in on the scale of wealth compared with other families. In that case, take the opportunity to explain that different occupations pay different salaries. That in turn can kick off a discussion of jobs and careers, such as why basketball players are paid more than teachers (see Chapter 12),

"I got a tricycle, Cindy got rollerblades; I got a bike, Cindy got a pony. I guess we're up to a car."

*Reprinted by permission of Andrew Toos*

why someone might want to be a writer rather than a doctor even though doctors earn more, or why being your own boss might be attractive.

Explain that some people might choose a lower-paying job because it suits their talents or gives them more satisfaction—or be forced into one because they don't have the skills or training for anything better. Now is a good time to make your pitch about getting a good education if your kids want to be able to

| Prices Then & Now | | |
|---|---|---|
| 1960 | Movie ticket | $ .86 |
| 1970 | Movie ticket | $2.03 |
| Present | Movie ticket | $4.18 |

*Prices reflect the average price of all tickets, both matinee and evening shows.*

*To adjust earlier prices to account for the effects of inflation, multiply 1960 price by 5 and 1970 price by 4.*

afford a big-screen TV or a trip to Disney World when they grow up.

Children need to hear an objective discussion about work. They'll become pretty cynical if all they hear is you or your spouse complaining about being overworked and underpaid. If your kids ask whether you make as much money as your boss, don't answer, "I wish," as if you're somehow being shortchanged. Better to respond, "No, but some-day *you* will."

CHAPTER 3

# "Why do you have to get a new job so far away and make us move? I don't want to leave my friends."

### You're tempted to say:
"Would you rather go to the poorhouse?"

### Dr. T's Rx:
Resist the temptation to be glib. What's a figure of speech to you is literal truth to your children. Even if your financial situation really is that precarious, there's such a thing as being *too* honest.

Instead, explain to the children that your new job will make it easier for your family to buy the things they need (including, presumably, things the

That's Life!

Consider a kid's-eye view of the world. Food appears on the table. There's always (well, almost always) another clean shirt in the closet. A car and driver chauffeur you from place to place. Flick a switch and the computer turns on. Flick another and you're watching Nickelodeon. Life is good. Life is cheap.

With so much taken care of for them, it's not surprising that children can't appreciate what it costs to keep a household running. It's little wonder that they can't understand why a new bike just doesn't fit into the family budget. To give them a glimpse into the real world (which might prove eye-opening for you, too), try playing the following version of "Let's pretend," suitable for children of about 10 years old and up:

"Let's pretend that you're 18 and on your own. You work full time at a fast-food restaurant making $5 an hour. That's $200 a week for 40 hours of work, or $800 a month—enough to buy quite a nice bike, right?

"But you won't actually take home $800, of course; after taxes, your pay will be more like $700. And, remember, you're on your own now, so you'll have to rent an apartment. [Check market rents in your local newspaper. For our purposes we'll use $350 a month.] You'll have to pay for electricity and heat—but let's give you a break and assume that utilities are included in the rent.

"Now you're down to $350, out of which you'll have to buy food. To keep things simple, figure that you'll spend about one-fourth of what we spend as a family of four, so your share is

32

kids want). Acknowledge that the move will be an adjustment for you, too, and even a little scary. But emphasize that you're all in this together. If you've been out of work for a while prior to the move, your children have probably sensed your tension and felt the financial pinch, and may actually be as relieved as you are that you've found work.

It's true, though, that long-distance moves get more difficult as your kids get older. "The ultimate nightmare is to take a kid away before senior year," says one child psychologist. If you're in that situation, try to defuse possible conflicts by letting your kids know as early as possible that a move is in the works and bringing them in on discussions about buying houses and choosing schools. You might even consider taking them with you on a scouting expedition to your new home.

*around $30 a week, or $120 a month. Remember, that's just groceries, not restaurant meals or pizzas!*

*"You'll want a phone to talk to your friends—and maybe, once in a while, your old mom and dad—so that's another $20 or so a month (not counting the installation fee of $30). Can't do without the cable? Subtract another $30 a month. (And you thought it came with the TV!)*

*"Let's see, now we're down to $180. You already have a car—after all, we're just pretending—but gasoline sets you back around $15 a week (we'll assume you learn how to change your own oil). There's also the not-so-small matter of car insurance, at $1,500-plus per year for someone who's still a teenager.*

*"Gong! Sorry, but you're in the hole already. And you haven't even gotten to the good stuff yet, like movies, clothes and CDs. You can forget the bicycle, unless you decide to ditch the car and pedal to work. On the other hand, you could get a higher paying job, which will require more education, so you may have to take out student loans. But that's life."*

Of course, your own family income is almost certainly higher than $800 a month, but so are your expenses. Even if you don't share the details of your household finances, running through an exercise like this can give your kids a frame of reference—and silence the pleas for a bike.

# "If you lose your job, how will we get money to buy food?"

### You're tempted to say:
"Don't worry about it. That's my problem."

### Dr. T's Rx:
You mean well, but you're actually being too reassuring. If your job's in jeopardy, of course your kids will worry. Even if they're not quite sure what it means to be unemployed, they can sense you're upset and they're going to pick up on your cues. It's easy for them to imagine that things are worse than they are.

Be as straight with them as you can about how a job loss might affect your finances, but don't burden them with problems they can't handle. You can tell them, for example, that you'll get money from unemployment benefits without telling them that those benefits will eventually run out. Tell them that many people nowadays lose or change their jobs, and explain how you're going to go about looking for a new one. Tell them you'll have to cut back on spending for a while, and ask for their suggestions.

Whatever you do, don't try to shield the children by continuing to spend money you can no longer afford. Kids are surprisingly adaptable to economic circumstances. A survey by the American Board of Family Practice showed that, to help their families through a financial crunch, a majority of teenagers were willing to get jobs, buy fewer clothes and give up some of their allowance.

## For Young Readers
• • • • • • • • • • • • • • • • • • • •

For elementary-school children, a couple of good books that deal with the subject of a parent losing a job are *Tight Times*, by Barbara Shook Hazen (Puffin Books), and *Ramona and Her Father*, by Beverly Cleary (Avon Camelot).

# Gifts & Money Manners

**F**or children, parents aren't the only source of cash and goodies. Other families invite them to the movies. Relatives send them money. Grandparents are particularly generous. One study found that in a typical month about half of all the grandparents surveyed had bought gifts for their grandchildren. On average, they spent $82 per grandchild for major holidays, $42 for birthdays and $19 for lesser holidays such as Valentine's Day.

But such largess doesn't come without strings attached. Textbooks will tell you that money has several uses. It's a medium of exchange, for example, and a store of value. In the real world money is also a social ritual, and children are often baffled by the niceties of financial etiquette. When you receive a gift, do you have to write a thank-you note or is a spoken thank you okay? Do your grandparents expect you to put your birthday check in the bank, or can you spend it? Should you accept your friend's offer to buy your movie ticket or pay for your own?

After witnessing his parents and another couple spar over who would pick up a dinner tab, one puzzled 10-year-old observed, "If someone offered to pay for me, I'd sure let them." Often it's okay to accept an offer like that. But your kids need to know when to fold and when to hold out for the check.

# "Can I buy Jenny a new bike [or any other expensive gift] for her birthday? She really wants one."

### You're tempted to say:

"Don't be silly. That's way too expensive."

### Dr. T's Rx:

It may sound silly to you, but your child is quite serious. To young children who don't yet grasp the abstract idea of money and price, one gift costs about as much as another. So they might as well get what their friends want most.

Let your children down gently by telling them that a new bicycle is the kind of special present that Jenny's parents might like to buy for her. Then steer your kids toward smaller gifts with lower price tags.

If your children are older, tell them what you think is an appropriate price to pay for a birthday gift—in Dr. T's opinion, $10 to $20. Kids may want to exceed that in the case of a special friend, but remind them that price isn't the only factor. The friend might be embarrassed by a gift that's too expensive—and the friend's parents might feel obliged to reciprocate, even if they can't afford it.

Older kids who are given the responsibility of buying birthday gifts with their own allowance money catch on quickly. "Instead of just going to the store and randomly selecting something, Luke thought a little more about the person he was buying for," one mother says of her 12-year-old. "In one case he remembered that his classmate was artistic, so he purchased drawing paper, colored pencils and markers. It was the recipient's favorite gift."

# "Can I ask Grandma for a new [fill in the blank with any expensive gift that Mom and Dad aren't willing to buy]?"

**You're tempted to say:**
"It can't hurt."

### Dr. T's Rx:

Putting the squeeze on Grandma is tacky, and puts *her* on the spot if she doesn't want to buy the expensive gift either, or can't afford it.

Tell your kids it would probably give Grandma more pleasure to surprise them with a gift of her own choosing. If Grandma would like some hints—and some grandparents do—you could offer a wish list, but it should include a variety of gifts in different price ranges so that she could take her pick.

For their part, grandparents shouldn't let their children and grandchildren come to expect that they'll always show up bearing expensive gifts. Grandparents love to buy stuff for their grandkids, but it's possible to be generous to a fault—as in the case of the 5-year-old whose grandmother bought her 55—count 'em, 55—outfits at one time, or the 6-year-old whose grandparents sent him a combination TV/VCR. Spontaneous surprises are fine, but in the interest of not over-indulging, parents and grandparents should consult ahead of time about major purchases. Grandparents shouldn't feel obliged to hand over mega-presents, and parents should have better manners than to ask.

> ## Money Talks
> • • • • • • • • • • • • • • • • • • • • • • • •
>
> Since the 1920s, "slug" has meant a nickel or dime-sized counterfeit coin, which people tried to use in subway turnstiles or pay phones.

# "Can I spend the money I got for my birthday?"

### You're tempted to say:
"Give it to me and I'll take care of it."

### Dr. T's Rx:

In general, kids should be allowed to keep and spend the money they get as gifts. That's probably what the gift-giver would want, along with a report on what the kids bought. Nothing is less gratifying and more frustrating to a child than money that arrives in the mail and is promptly whisked away by Mom or Dad.

But it's understandable if you don't want your 5-year-old dropping $50 at the toy store. So Dr. T offers a multiple-choice answer, based on your child's age and the amount of the gift:

| Prices Then & Now | | |
|---|---|---|
| 1960 | Barbie™ doll | $ 3.00 |
| 1970 | Barbie™ doll | $ 7.00 |
| Present | Barbie™ doll | $10.00 |

*To adjust earlier prices to account for the effects of inflation, multiply 1960 price by 5 and 1970 price by 4.*

*Prices courtesy of Mattel, Inc.*

- **One:** Preschoolers are allowed to spend gifts of up to $20 (when accompanied by you, of course), which would buy a character Barbie doll or an action toy. Anything above that is saved for another day. Another option is to let the little ones spend cash gifts, while you save the checks.

- **Two:** Six to 12-year-olds, with more expensive tastes and a better-developed sense of how much things cost, get to spend gifts of up to $50, which might buy a new soccer bag or a baseball glove.

- **Three:** Teenagers have discretion over gifts of up to $100.

Regardless of age, gifts over $100 demand some

parental input. One dad whose son occasionally gets gifts of $200 from his grandmother requires that his son spend $50 to $100 on something he needs—a new winter jacket, for example. With an amount that large, gift-givers might consider consulting with you ahead of time to designate how the money should be spent.

A word about gifts of money: They're both appropriate and appreciated. Dr. T doesn't know many children above the age of 5 or so who would turn up their noses at cash. In the words of one 6-year-old, "Money is importanter than toys. I can buy things with it."

For very young children, checks aren't much fun because the kids can't play with them, spend them or cash them by themselves. Grandparents sending checks could also enclose a couple of crisp dollar bills.

**"I don't have to be a good boy for the tooth fairy, and HE still comes through!"**

*Dennis The Menace® used by permission of Hank Ketcham and © by North America Syndicate.*

# "I lost the $10 Aunt Barbara sent me for my birthday. What should I do?"

### You're tempted to say:

"You wouldn't have lost it if you had put it in the bank."

### Dr. T's Rx:

While you're technically correct, there's no reason to require your kids to put an amount that small in the bank.

On the other hand, your children do have a responsibility to take care of their own money, so don't feel you have to give them a chance to earn it back by doing extra chores. Let them eat the loss, and tell them that next time they will have to be more careful.

They probably will learn their lesson if it's a check that has been misplaced. Eventually Aunt Barbara will notice that the check hasn't been cashed, and your child will have to 'fess up.

## Prices Then & Now

|         | Big Mac | Regular fries | 12 oz. soda |
|---------|---------|---------------|-------------|
| 1970    | $ .55   | $ .20         | $ .12       |
| 1980    | $1.08   | $ .45         | $ .45       |
| Present | $1.84   | $ .77         | $ .89       |

*To adjust earlier prices to account for the effects of inflation, multiply 1970 prices by 4 and 1980 prices by 1.75.*

*Prices courtesy of McDonald's Inc.*

# "The sweaters Uncle Bill sends for Christmas every year are always too small. Can't I ask for money this year?"

### You're tempted to say:

"That sounds tacky. And besides, it will hurt his feelings."

### Dr. T's Rx:

Like putting the gift squeeze on Grandma, *asking* Uncle Bill for money is tacky. *Suggesting* that Uncle Bill send the kids money in lieu of another gift is a reasonable request.

Explain to him that as the children are getting older it's difficult even for you to buy things that fit and that the kids like. If you don't want to make an out-and-out request for cash, suggest instead a gift certificate for a book, music or clothing store. Or remind Uncle Bill to include a gift voucher or some other proof of purchase so you can exchange the item for another size if it doesn't fit.

Who knows? Uncle Bill may actually be relieved. It's possible that for all these years your kids have been getting too-small sweaters or fire engine pajamas because Uncle Bill felt obligated to send a gift but didn't know what to buy—and thought that sending cash would seem tacky. It isn't fair to let him keep frittering away his money on presents that aren't being used.

Every family seems to have a relative whose gifts are the subject of good-humored jokes. But good manners are no laughing matter, and your kids should always thank the giver for his or her thoughtfulness, even if the sweater is too tight or the pajamas have fire engines on them.

> *Remind the kids that the size of a present has nothing to do with the amount of love that comes with it.*

# "Why does Grandma Pearl give bigger presents than Grandma Rose?"

### You're tempted to say:
"Because Grandma Pearl has more money."

### Dr. T's Rx:
Honesty is a good policy, but don't make too big a deal about any difference in wealth. You may be more sensitive about it than the kids, who are probably just being curious and not passing judgment.

Remind the kids that the size of a present has nothing to do with the amount of love that comes with it, although Dr. T suspects that kids intuitively know this. In Dr. T's experience, what children really value are grandparents who are interested in the kids' activities, joke with them and share special interests that don't need to cost much money. The following grandparents get Dr. T's commendation for giving inexpensive but cherished presents:

- **The grandfather who made a scrapbook of favorite comic strips** he read to the kids when they came to visit. When they outgrew the comics, he presented them with the book as a memento.

- **The grandmother who regularly sent her grandson newspaper clippings** about her hometown hockey team. Her grandson was a big fan, but lived in another city where the team didn't get much coverage.

- **The grandparents who sent their grandchildren rolls of postage stamps** with a request that the kids use the stamps to send some of their school papers.

- **The grandmother who started a tradition of giving her younger grandchildren storybooks** with a homemade tape of her voice reading the story. The kids particularly liked her directives to "Turn the page."

## "When two grown-ups go out to eat, why does one of them offer to pay the bill and the other say no? If someone wanted to buy lunch for me, I'd sure let them."

*Picking up a tab on the spur of the moment often puts the other person on the spot.*

### You're tempted to say:
"You'll understand when you get older."

### Dr. T's Rx:
Admit it. Plenty of grown-ups would love to accept an offer of a free lunch. But more than money is at stake here. You might call it a matter of table manners. Check etiquette is something kids need to learn just as much as they need to learn not to slurp their soup or eat peas with a knife.

Explain to your children that treating a friend to a meal is a great idea. Maybe you'd do it because it's your friend's birthday, or as a way of saying thanks for something nice that he or she has done for you.

But it's always best to make clear *ahead* of time that you're going to pick up the tab. Making the offer on the spur of the moment often puts the other person on the spot. Your friend doesn't know if you really *want* to pay or if you're just trying to be polite. That's why lots of adults turn down the offer of a free meal. Unless you've agreed in advance that one of you is going to treat, assume that you'll each be paying your own way.

If the other person strenuously insists on picking up the check, it's better to say yes than to make a scene over the spaghetti.

# "Do I have to write a thank-you note to Grandma for my birthday gift?"

### You're tempted to say:

"Well, maybe a phone call will do."

### Dr. T's Rx:

Yes, maybe a phone call *will* do. Every gift deserves a thank you in some form, and it's worth nagging your kids to offer one. You want to make them feel so guilty that they'll eventually remember to say thanks on their own and will one day nag their own children. A spontaneously written note is certainly the most desirable outcome.

But as a parent Dr. T knows that when a thank-you note isn't immediately forthcoming it doesn't necessarily mean that kids (and their parents) are ungrateful, just that in the rush of daily living the task of writing one sometimes gets put off. On the theory that a spoken thank you is better than none, Dr. T is willing to risk the ire of manners mavens and suggest these rules of thank-you etiquette for kids, updated for the information age:

- **If children receive a gift in person, they should thank the giver verbally on the spot.** In the case of a birthday party, the parents of the birthday child should also thank the other parents when they come to pick up their kids.

- **If children receive a gift in the mail, a telephoned thank you—or even an e-mail message—is acceptable,**

## Small Change
● ● ● ● ● ● ● ● ● ● ● ● ● ● ● ● ● ● ● ● ● ●

Did you ever notice that the dollar sign looks like an "S" with one or two lines through it?

Look at the dollar sign carefully. You'll see that the curves in the "S" and the line through it combine to make the letter "P" twice, once facing left at the top and the other facing right at the bottom. The "P" stands for the Spanish peso, one of many foreign coins that were circulated in the early American colonies. Eventually the symbol came to be adopted for the U.S. dollar.

especially if the giver is someone you talk to frequently. Lots of grandparents carry on satisfying relationships via e-mail with their long-distance grandchildren.

- **A formal written thank-you is still in order if the gift is an especially generous one,** or if the occasion is a special one, such as a graduation. A note is also a must if friends or relatives have extended their hospitality by taking the kids on a trip or inviting them for a visit. Children can create cards on a computer or, in a real pinch, buy pre-written notes at the stationery store so all they have to do is fill in the blanks.

A note to grandparents and other gift-givers: There's an old saying that you should never lend a family member money and expect to get it back. Dr. T would add that you should never give a family member a gift and expect to get a thank-you note. Thanks in any of the forms listed above will do. If you never hear a word in any form, show this book to your adult children!

Make the most of the thanks you get. One grandmother framed a note from her grandson and hung it on the dining-room wall—a painless yet effective reminder to him that such courtesies are appreciated.

Calvin and Hobbs © 1995 Watterson. Dist. by UNIVERSAL PRESS SYNDICATE. Reprinted with permission. All rights reserved.

# "Can we invite Kathleen to go to the movies with us this afternoon?"

(Asked with Kathleen staring longingly over your child's shoulder)

### You're tempted to say:
"Sure, why not?"

### Dr. T's Rx:

It's okay to extend a spur-of-the-moment invitation, but be prepared to pay for your guest. Neither Kathleen nor her parents have planned for the expense and might not have enough money on hand to cover it.

For future reference, tell your kids that if they want to take a friend along on an excursion that costs money, they should call the night before to extend the invitation. That way you can tell the other parents if the treat's on you, or, if not, what the approximate cost will be. That gives them an opportunity either to decline gracefully or to send their kids prepared to pay.

## Prices Then & Now

|          | Newsweek | Seventeen | Sports Illustrated | Archie Comics |
|----------|----------|-----------|--------------------|---------------|
| 1960s    | $ .35    | $ .50     | $ .35              | $ .15         |
| 1970s    | $ .75    | $ .75     | $ .75              | $ .25         |
| 1980s    | $1.95    | $1.50     | $1.95              | $ .65         |
| Present  | $2.95    | $3.25     | $2.95              | $1.50         |

*To adjust earlier prices to account for the effects of inflation, multiply 1960s prices by 5; 1970s prices by 3 and 1980s prices by 1.5.*

# "I'd like to invite Andy/Andrea to the dance on Saturday night. Do I have to pay for both of us?"

### You're tempted to say:

"I don't care *who* pays as long as it isn't me."

### Dr. T's Rx:

Kids always do better with specific guidelines. Call Dr. T old-fashioned, but here's her first rule of dating etiquette: He or she who does the asking should pick up the tab. Dr. T's second rule of dating etiquette: He or she who picks up the tab should do it with his or her own money. (One exception might be an expensive event, such as a prom; see Chapter 10).

In a dating situation, it's bad form to say, "I'd like to invite you to the movies on Saturday night, but I don't have any money so you'll have to pay." Kids (and adults) should wait till they have the money before issuing the invitation. Or they can go in a group where no one pairs off and everyone goes Dutch.

If your child is on the receiving end of the invitation, it wouldn't hurt to bring along extra cash just in case his or her date hasn't heard about Dr. T's rules of dating etiquette.

# "You told me to pay my own way into the amusement park, but Mr. Haynes wouldn't take my money. What should I have done?"

**You're tempted to say:**
"You shouldn't have let him pay."

**Dr. T's Rx:**

In any showdown between an adult and a child, the child's natural inclination is to back off. Teach your kids the art of reciprocation. If their host pays for their admission, the kids could offer to treat everyone to ice cream, for example. It may not be an even exchange if the ice cream costs less than the tickets, but making the gesture is what counts.

When your kids are invited on an excursion with another family, assume that the other family is only going to furnish transportation and that your kids will be taking care of their own meals and other expenses. If there's any doubt about who's going to pay, discuss it with the other parents ahead of time. If the other parents are going to pick up the tab, make sure your kids have their own pocket money to buy souvenirs or other extras—and to treat everyone to ice cream.

If you're the one who's issuing the invitation, you can avoid any misunderstandings by telling the parents what you intend to pay for. And when your guests offer to buy you an ice cream cone, don't turn them down.

# Kids as Customers

**K**ids don't always spend *your* money. Once in a while they spend their own. But just because they're old enough to participate in the world of commerce doesn't mean they understand how it works. When they're young, their naivete can be endearing; as they get older, it can be expensive.

Children are likely to be intimidated by adult salesclerks, who might (they fear) take advantage of kids. They're self-conscious about counting out their cash and worry that they might get the wrong change. They're tempted to buy the first thing they see instead of shopping around for the best price. And they don't know what to do if their purchase doesn't fit, doesn't work, or breaks shortly after they get it home.

Whatever your kids' age, they probably know less than you think they do about handling money. So it pays to belabor what, to an adult, might seem to be obvious.

# "Can I use my money to buy a candy bar?"

(Your preschooler waving a $10 bill)

### You're tempted to say:

"With that much money you could buy *ten* candy bars."

### Dr. T's Rx:

Nice try, but don't be surprised if your child doesn't get it. Preschoolers don't think in abstract terms. To young children, all paper money is the same. Four quarters are preferable to a dollar bill because there are more of them (and they spin), and a nickel is better than a dime because it's bigger.

Simplify your tactics. Tell your kids that a $10 bill is much more than they need for one candy bar and that they should save it to buy other things. Then help them count out the exact change they'll need.

If the kids are still a little fuzzy about how much things cost, don't worry. At least they understand that money can be exchanged for other things, which is about as much as you can hope for at this age. They'll pick up the more abstract concepts when they start to learn about money in school.

"When you don't have any money, EVERYTHING is high-priced."

*Dennis The Menace® used by permission of Hank Ketcham and © by North America Syndicate.*

# "The hair ribbon I bought at the dollar store cost one dollar, so why did I have to pay an extra nickel?"

### You're tempted to say:
"That's your government at work."

### Dr. T's Rx:
Save the editorial comments at least until you've explained the concept of sales tax: what it is, who collects it and what it's used for. Otherwise, your kids will draw their own conclusions, which are often way off the mark: "The storekeeper gets to keep it," one child told Dr. T. "The store uses it to buy new things to sell," said another. A third child was convinced that the money "goes to the President in Washington."

---

## Money Talks

Ever hear the phrase, "Not one red cent?" Well, "red cent" refers to the reddish color of the one-cent piece (which was originally made of copper).

---

If sales tax in your area is earmarked for a specific purpose and you know what that is, so much the better. Otherwise, you can get away with a couple of general statements, such as "Sales tax is extra money collected by the state (or local) government when you buy something. The government uses it to help pay its bills and provide services."

Your kids might be interested to know that not everything is taxed. Food bought in grocery stores is often exempt, and sometimes clothing as well. The amount of sales tax varies from state to state, and not every state charges one. Save any philosophical discussions about the merits of a sales tax versus an income tax until your kids are at least in junior high.

*Losing is a fact of life best learned by experience (and your kids will be less inclined to buy lottery tickets when they grow up).*

## "There's a contest on TV, and the prize is a trip to Disney World. Can I enter so we can go?"

### You're tempted to say:
"Don't bother. Nobody ever wins those things."

### Dr. T's Rx:

It's true your kids will almost certainly not win any contest they enter, but hope springs eternal. Explain to your children that with a limited number of prizes and lots of entrants the odds are against them. But let them enter anyway. Losing is a fact of life best learned by experience (and your kids will be less inclined to buy lottery tickets when they grow up).

One woman recalls her own childhood experience with games of chance. "One day my dad decided he would teach me to play poker. Once I had mastered the game, he suggested that we play for pennies. With the innocence of youth (and, I must confess, a touch of greed), I quickly agreed. Dad proceeded to clean me out. I was shocked. He later gave me back the coins, along with a lecture on get-rich-quick schemes and the risks of gambling. But what I remember most vividly was the feeling in my stomach when Dad won all my pennies."

Some contests are more child-friendly than others. The best of them should be easy to enter, have better odds than one in a million, and award lots of prizes instead of one big one. Kids should be able to write in for a list of winners. For many children, losing isn't as much of a disappointment as not knowing who won. Here's an excerpt from a letter written by one 9-year-old to the television show "Ghostwriter:" "I entered the 'Ghostwriter' sweepstakes last year. After I sent it in I never heard from you again. I wasn't sure when you were going to pick the winners and I was upset." The letter-writer was rewarded with a personal response, and a Ghostwriter pen and poster.

If the contest requires your children to write or draw something, or otherwise expend some constructive effort, entering could be a worthwhile experience regardless of the outcome.

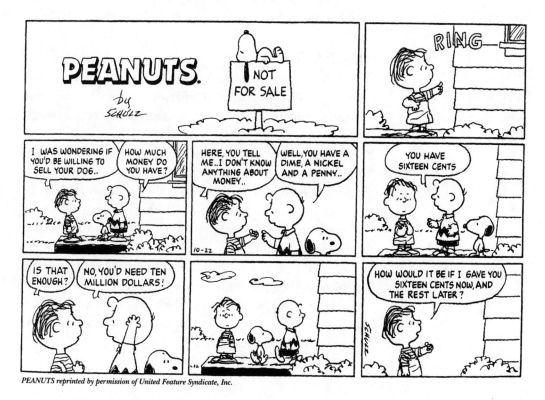

*PEANUTS reprinted by permission of United Feature Syndicate, Inc.*

# "When I pay for something, how do I know they won't cheat me just 'cause I'm a kid?"

**You're tempted to say:**

"Always count your change."

### Dr. T's Rx:

Don't assume that children know how to count change. They may be frantically trying to subtract numbers in their head, unaware that there's a much easier way.

If they buy something that costs $3.63, for example, and they hand the clerk a $5 bill, tell them to count the change from the smallest denomination to the largest: two pennies to make 65 cents, then a dime to make 75 cents, a quarter to make $4, and a dollar bill to make $5.

This system isn't intuitive. One woman sheepishly confesses that she didn't figure it out until she was a teenager and got her first job working the cash register at a bakery. (For more tips on how to handle cash, see the list on the opposite page.)

## Listen to Your Mother

"How to count change" (on the preceding page) was the first of what Dr. T had intended to be a list of ten tips for kids on how to feel comfortable about handling cash in public or buying something on their own. The idea was to ask grownups to contribute the best advice their own parents ever gave them on how to avoid losing their money or being cheated. But so many adults weighed in that the top ten became the lucky thirteen. Here are the rest, with compliments to contributors and their parents:

**2. Always stuff your dollar bills deep in your pocket so they don't fall out when you reach in for a coin or bus token.** Better yet, stuff them into a wallet or change purse, which you're less likely to pull out by mistake.

**3. When ordering at a fast-food restaurant, round off the menu prices to estimate your total.** That way you'll know you've been overcharged in case the clerk goofs and hits the Big Mac key twice.

**4. Don't break the big bills.** If your purchase comes to $9, pay with four ones and a five instead of a $10 bill. Once big bills are broken, you have a tendency to spend the money.

**5. Spend the crummy bills** and save the good ones for vending machines.

**6. Always pay the pennies.** If the price comes to $3.63 and you have a $5 bill and a handful of change, pay the three cents so that you don't get more pennies in change.

**7. Ditto above, but with paper money.** Suppose your purchase comes to $11 and you have a $20 bill and several ones. Give the clerk $21 so that you get a $10 bill in change. It's less cumbersome, and follows Tip no. 4 to save the larger bill.

**8. If you have to use a big bill to pay for a small purchase, tell the clerk verbally—** "Here's a twenty"—so there's no confusion. A good salesclerk should keep the bill out of the cash register until you get your change.

**9. Clean out your pockets or purse each day** and toss the coins into a savings jar. One man still follows this rule as an adult, and his spare change adds up to $40 to $60 a month, which he deposits in the bank or uses to treat himself to a nice dinner at a restaurant.

**10. Don't take all your money to the movies or the mall.** Take along only as much as you need to make your purchase. That way you don't risk leaving your life savings in your seat, or frittering it away at the candy counter. (And you won't have to worry about making change!)

**11. Don't shove a pile of crumpled bills onto the counter** and expect the salesclerk to sort them out. After the age of six or so, that stops being cute and starts becoming an annoyance to the clerk and the other people waiting in line—not to mention an invitation to be ripped off.

**12. If you're out with your parents and want one of them to hold onto your money, make sure it's in a separate wallet.** Loose bills and coins have a habit of getting mixed up with a parent's own funds, never to be sorted out.

**13. Don't put money in your mouth,** because you don't know where it's been. Actually, you *do* know where it's been, which is an even better reason not to put it in your mouth!

# "The antenna on my new remote-control car is broken. What should I do?"

### You're tempted to say:
"I *told* you that car wouldn't last."

### Dr. T's Rx:
If a toy has broken through no fault of their own, children should do the same things you would do if you bought something that didn't work: Call the manufacturer's 800 number, if one is available, or take the item back (even if it means an extra trip to the store on your part).

Kids are consumers, too, and are entitled to the same remedies as grown-ups if they're dissatisfied with a product. But they don't know the ropes and often feel at the mercy of adults. So you'll have to give them some basic tips—for example, always save the sales receipt—and go with them to return the item until they build more confidence.

"I accuse you of fiscal irresponsibility."

Farris/Cartoonists & Writers Syndicate

# "Toys 'R' Us has a great deal on the bike I've been saving for. Will you lend me the rest of the money I need so I can buy it now?"

### You're tempted to say:
"If it's that good a deal, why not?"

### Dr. T's Rx:

Go ahead and advance the money. Dr. T is a softie and appreciates a good bargain—especially if your child was smart enough to spot it in the first place. Just remember to set up a timetable for your child to repay the loan.

Should you charge interest? Not necessarily. You are, after all, a parent and not a banker. If you want to teach your kids about interest, charge a nominal amount, but nothing that's too onerous or too difficult for you to keep track of. If you're lending your son $20, for instance, you might charge him a flat 5%, or $1, to be added on to the last payment instead of collected in dribs and drabs while the loan is outstanding.

# "I signed up with a music club to get free CDs, but they keep sending me stuff and I can't pay for it. Will you bail me out or do I have to go to jail?"

### You're tempted to say:

"You should know better than to think you could get something for nothing."

### Dr. T's Rx:

That approach might have worked if your child had come to you before he or she joined the club, but kids generally don't. Now you have to deal with a pile of CDs and a stack of unpaid bills. Fortunately, neither of you will have to go to jail.

First, return the CDs. Then write the club a letter explaining that your child is a minor and signed up without your knowledge. The club will probably let you off the hook. In general, minors (usually those under the age of 18) can disavow contracts like these, and their parents (or other legal guardians) can't be held responsible, so the club won't press the point.

Some kids (and adults) get tripped up on "negative option" plans, which automatically send you a CD and bill you for it unless you return it. If your child really wants to continue his or her membership, you may be able to get the club to switch to a positive option plan, in which your child would be sent only those CDs that he or she specifically ordered. But your child would first have to fulfill the initial commitment to buy a certain number of CDs. (FYI: This strategy can also work for adults who are members of music or book clubs.)

Often parents aren't aware that their kids are piling up debts until dunning letters start arriving.

Don't be intimidated by fancy legal stationery. Write back and explain that your child is a minor, and the letters should stop.

Kids sometimes figure they'll outsmart the system by ordering the free CDs without any intention of buying any more. Even though it's possible to bail out because they're minors, they should never get the idea that it's okay to renege on a deal. At the very least you're going to have to spend your time doing battle with the music club's computer system to square your kids' account.

And it's just plain wrong. The kids should have to send back all their ill-gotten CDs, and you should consider imposing your own penalty, like pulling the plug on the CD player.

# The Color of Money

**K**ids think in concrete terms, so it's little wonder that many of the questions they ask about money involve currency and coins. "Why does all our money have to be green?" they want to know, or "Why is a nickel bigger than a dime?"

Grownups, of course, take money for granted and are generally clueless about its origins. "Because that's the way it's always been" is your natural response to your kids' questions.

And you're not far off the mark. In addition to being a medium of exchange (meaning that you can buy things with it), money is also a store of value (meaning that people are willing to hold on to it because they think it's worth something). To keep the public's confidence over the years, money has to be stable and reliable. That's why you won't see the Treasury changing the green in greenbacks to jade or teal, just because that happens to be the color du jour.

But 'fess up. Even grownups wonder from time to time why we call a dollar a "buck," or for that matter, who decided that the dollar would be the official currency of the U.S. In this chapter you'll get a glimpse into the colorful past of U.S. coins and currency, and the fascinating history of the language of money.

# "Do we have to use coins as money, or could we use something else?"

### *Dr. T:*

People can use—and historically have used— almost anything as money, as long as it's recognized as valuable. Yap Islanders in the South Pacific used huge wheels carved of a special stone that was brought hundreds of miles over the open ocean. Native Americans used necklaces made of shells, which were called wampum; the darker the shell, the more valuable the necklace. Coins were finally settled on because the metal was valuable (many early U.S. coins were made of gold and silver), malleable (meaning it could be worked into different shapes and designs) and portable (it was easy to carry in your pocket).

# "Why is a nickel bigger than a dime if a dime is worth more?"

### *Dr. T:*

It goes back to when "major" U.S. coins—the dollar, half-dollar, quarter and dime—were made of silver. The half-dollar, quarter and dime were made in proportion to the dollar in size and weight. So the half-dollar was half the size of the dollar, the quarter was one-fourth as large as the dollar, and so on.

The nickel and the penny weren't made out of silver so their size didn't matter. They were considered minor coins—small change, you might say—and at one time could legally be used to pay only very small debts.

# "Why is a penny made of copper?"

## Dr. T:

Actually, it isn't—or not much, anyway. A penny is only 2.5% copper; the other 97.5% is zinc. It used to be the other way around (95% copper and 5% zinc), but in the early 1980s the value of the copper in the coin was beginning to approach the penny's face value. So the U.S. Mint, the U.S. Treasury agency that makes coins, changed the composition of the cent.

Why wasn't the penny made of silver, like other coins? We don't know for sure, although probably because it wasn't considered a major coin. The first cents were minted in 1792 and they've been made of copper in some form ever since, except for the year 1943 during World War II, when copper was needed for the war effort. That year, pennies were made out of zinc-coated steel.

But pennies haven't always looked the same. They used to be bigger than today's version. The first "small cent," which is the size of the current coin, was minted in 1856. And today's Lincoln penny first appeared in 1909, when it was issued to commemorate the 100th year of the president's birth.

---

## Small Change

● ● ● ● ● ● ● ● ● ● ● ● ● ● ● ● ● ● ● ● ● ● ●

- **A nickel is only 25% nickel**; the other 75% is copper. In fact, a nickel has far more copper than a copper penny (see the question on this page).
- **There's no such coin as a penny**; its official title is the cent. Penny is a colloquialism that goes back to the English word pence. And there's no such coin as a nickel, either. Officially, it's a five-cent piece, or a half-dime.

# "On the penny, why is Lincoln facing toward the right while presidents on other coins are facing left?"

### Dr. T:

It's not a political statement, it's just the way the artist happened to design the coin.

# "Why do some coins have ridges around the outside?"

### Dr. T:

In the old days, when coins were literally "worth their weight" in silver or gold, people sometimes cheated by filing the edges of the coins and saving the precious metal. The ridges—called reeds—were adopted to discourage filing and to foil counterfeiting. Nowadays reeded edges help sight-impaired people tell one coin from another. The penny and the dime are similar in size, for example, so the reeded edges on a dime make it easier to identify.

"Where's the engine?"

## "Is my silver dollar really made out of silver?"

### Dr. T:

Not unless your coin dates back to the 1930s. That's the last time a 90% silver dollar was minted. No silver dollars were issued between 1936 and 1970. The last two dollar coins—the Eisenhower dollar, minted from 1971 to 1978, and the Susan B. Anthony dollar (1979 to 1981)—are "sandwich coins" like the dime, quarter and half-dollar, made with a pure copper center, and coated with a mixture of copper and nickel.

---

### Small Change

• • • • • • • • • • • • • • • • • • • • • • • • •

In the old days coins were valued for their precious metals–either gold or silver. Today they're valued for their electromagnetic properties so they can be used in vending machines. That's why they're made of a copper–nickel alloy.

---

## "Can I use one of my silver dollars to pay for an ice cream bar?"

### Dr. T:

You can—but the Good Humor vendor doesn't have to take it. All coins are legal tender, meaning they can be used to buy things or pay debts. But the law doesn't *require* anyone to accept coins as payment. Every once in a while, for instance, you may hear about someone who thinks he or she has been unfairly ticketed for a traffic violation and pays the fine with a carload of pennies. But the joke's on the driver; the traffic court doesn't have to accept the coins.

## "Is it true that the government is going to issue a new dollar coin made out of gold?"

*A coin in normal use can last 30 years.*

### Dr. T:

Congress is talking about issuing a new dollar coin that would be gold-colored and have smooth edges (to distinguish it from the quarter). But it wouldn't be made of gold. And it might not be made at all. Vending-machine operators and transit systems like the idea of replacing dollar bills with coins. The Chicago Transit Authority collects 325,000 bills a day and employs 20 workers just to straighten out dog-eared dollars. But Americans might not like the idea of carrying around more change and less currency.

## "How long do coins last?"

### Dr. T:

A coin in normal use can last 30 years. Coins are classified in three categories: "current," which are regular circulating coins; "uncurrent," which are worn but still recognizable and machine-countable; and "mutilated" which are unrecognizable, corroded, broken, bent, fused together or otherwise not machine-countable. If you have coins in that last category you can send them to the U. S. Mint in Philadelphia, which will redeem them by the pound at close to face value (write to the U.S. Mint, Coin Redemption Branch, 101 N. Fifth Street, Philadelphia, PA 19106). But you have to send no less than one pound of coins, separated by denomination. The Mint won't redeem individual coins.

# "How many new coins are made every year?"

## *Dr. T:*

Here's how they stack up on average: pennies, 14 billion; nickels, dimes and quarters, one to two billion each; half-dollars, between 30 and 40 million.

There's no ceiling on the number of coins that can be struck; the Mint will produce whatever is demanded. The total value of coins in circulation is a little over $20 billion—compared with more than $455 billion in currency.

Sometimes the Mint has to produce more coins even though there seem to be plenty outstanding, because a certain number of coins are lost or taken out of circulation—like that jar of pennies sitting on your closet floor. At the end of 1990 the government conducted a coin census and figured there were 132 billion cents in circulation. Since then the Mint has produced billions more of the coins. Yet a few years ago there was actually a shortage of pennies, and the government had to appeal to Americans to get those cents out of their jars and back into circulation. (If you want to turn in your pennies to a bank, you may have to roll them first—a task that's tedious for parents but is a fun way to occupy kids, especially if they're allowed keep the value of the coins they turn in.)

---

## *Small Change*
● ● ● ● ● ● ● ● ● ● ● ● ● ● ● ● ● ● ● ● ● ● ● ●

The "heads" side of a coin is called the obverse; the "tails" side is called the reverse. The Lincoln Memorial is pictured on the reverse of a penny; on a nickel it's Monticello, Thomas Jefferson's home in Virginia; on the dime, it's the torch (liberty), olive branch (peace) and oak branch (strength); on the quarter, an eagle; and on the half-dollar the Presidential coat of arms.

## "Who needs pennies, anyway? Why don't we just get rid of them?"

*Among current coins, the design of the Lincoln penny has been in circulation the longest, dating back to 1909.*

### Dr. T:

Congress has considered such a proposal, but it has never gone anywhere, mostly because of opposition from the states. For state revenue collectors, pennies are crucial when setting sales tax rates; it's much easier to raise the sales tax by a penny than by a nickel. And if the rate is, say, 4% or 7%, pennies are critical to collecting the right amount of tax.

## "Who decides which person should appear on each coin?"

### Dr. T:

All those decisions are made by act of Congress and the Treasury Department. The Secretary of the Treasury has some discretionary power to change the design of coins, but has always left that up to Congress. If Congress isn't specific about how it wants a coin to look, the U.S. Mint can decide or, if there's time, even sponsor a design contest. The portrait of Thomas Jefferson on the nickel was chosen after a design competition among 390 artists in 1938.

Among current coins, the design of the Lincoln penny has been in circulation the longest, dating back to 1909, when it was introduced on the 100th anniversary of Lincoln's birth. Washington began appearing on the quarter in 1932, the 200th anniversary of his birth. In the case of Franklin D. Roosevelt (the dime) and John F. Kennedy (the half-dollar), it was each man's untimely death in office that prompted his almost immediate commemoration on U.S. coins.

# "If I find a really dirty old coin, is it worth a lot of money?"

## Dr. T:

Probably not. Remember, the average coin is in circulation for 30 years, so even if you find a penny that was issued 30 years ago (which sounds like ancient times to most kids) it isn't old by coin standards. On the other hand, you aren't likely to find a coin minted prior to 30 years ago, because most of those have been taken out of circulation by collectors. What you've probably found is a dirty coin made relatively recently that is worth its face value and nothing more.

But just in case . . . *don't* clean the coin, especially if you can't read the date. If it really is old, you'll decrease it's value substantially if you polish it up. If you can't make out the date, have it examined by at least two different coin dealers. You can also get an opinion from the American Numismatic Association, 818 North Cascade Ave., Colorado Springs, CO 80903–3279.

If the date is readable and it's older than 30 years, look up the coin in the *Guidebook of United States Coins*, the so-called "Red Book" that is published every year and is the bible of coin collectors. Remember, though, that just because a coin is old doesn't necessarily mean it's worth a lot. Age isn't the only thing that determines a coin's value; rarity, condition and demand are important, too. A worn Indianhead penny from the early 1900s might be worth $1. But a "proof" coin from the same era, distinguishable by its brilliant mirror-like surface and sharpness of detail, might fetch closer to $200.

## Small Change

● ● ● ● ● ● ● ● ● ● ● ● ● ● ● ● ● ● ● ● ● ● ● ● ●

The 1913 Liberty Head nickel is worth around a half-million dollars. But don't bother rummaging around in your pockets or piggy bank. Only five of the coins were struck.

# "If I start collecting coins, will I be able to sell my collection for a lot of money some day?"

### Dr. T:

Don't count on it. When it comes to collecting, you should do it for love, *not* money—and that advice applies to coins, comic books, sports cards, dolls and all other collectibles (see Chapter 9). While it's possible to make money, the market for any collectible can be complex and fickle. In 1995 kids were searching their pockets for the so-called doubled-die cent, a coin with an imperfection that made certain features appear to have been struck twice. The first few coins discovered sold for more than $1,000, but as more turned up the price quickly dropped to less than $100.

## Small Change

• • • • • • • • • • • • • • • • • • • • • • • •

Gold is stored in the form of bars that are a little smaller than building bricks but much heavier. Each gold bar weighs 400 troy ounces, or about 27.4 regular pounds.

On the other hand, collecting coins can be fun for kids because it doesn't take a lot of money to start buying coins that interest you—U.S. Civil War coins, worldwide coins with pictures of animals, or coins from a particular country, for example. You can even buy 2,000-year-old silver and copper coins for as little as $5 or $10 (for more information on coin collecting, write to the American Numismatic Association at the address on the preceding page).

Just don't expect that when you're 18 you'll be able to sell your collection for enough money to send yourself to Harvard. You might make the carfare—but not the tuition.

# "What do people mean when they say 'Do you think we're as rich as Fort Knox?'"

*Dr. T:*

Fort Knox is a former Army base near Louisville, Kentucky. Back in the 1930s the U.S. government built a gold depository there to hold most of the gold that was owned by the government and which, at the time, backed up the value of the U.S. dollar. The outer wall of the depository was made of granite and lined with concrete, as a symbol of national security and the soundness of the dollar, which was "as good as gold."

The government's stock of gold is still stored at Fort Knox, and has been stable for quite a few years at around 150 million troy ounces (a troy ounce is slightly heavier than a regular ounce). The price of an ounce of gold has been around $300 to $400 for years, but the U.S. gold reserves are carried on the books at $42.22 per ounce.

# "Does the U.S. government ever spend its gold?"

*Dr. T:*

Nope. The government *does* issue a gold coin. It's called the American Eagle, and it's intended for collectors and sold as an investment, not as legal tender. But, by law, the gold that goes into those coins must be newly mined in the U.S.

## "Do people still mine for gold?"

### Dr. T:

Sure. The U.S. produces around 11 million ounces a year, more than half of which come from Nevada and California. Despite the legendary Forty-Niners and the Gold Rush of 1849, the biggest growth in the U.S. gold industry has come since 1980. Miners no longer use pans and picks. Chemical processes extract minute gold particles from the ore.

Even with the new gold supplies that are mined each year, all the gold in the world would fill only half the Washington Monument.

*All the gold in the world would fill only half the Washington Monument.*

## "Who thought of using a dollar as the main unit of U.S. money?"

### Dr. T:

It was adopted by the Continental Congress in 1785, although the first dollar wasn't actually issued until a few years later (it was a coin, not a bill).

*Reprinted with special permission of King Features Syndicate.*

The Bureau of Engraving and Printing—the U.S. Treasury agency that prints money—washes bills over and over to test their durability.

## "How did they decide on the name 'dollar'?"

### Dr. T:

The word "dollar" actually dates back to 1518, when a large silver coin was minted in Bohemia in the valley (or "thal") of Joachim. Called the "Joachimsthaler," the coin spread across Europe, and its name was adapted to each country's language. In Dutch, for example, it was the "daalder," in Scandinavian the "daler" and in English the "dollar."

The Spanish peso, also called the Spanish milled dollar, was one of the principal coins in the early American colonies, along with traditional English money such as pounds and shillings. But once the U.S. declared its independence, the country gravitated toward the dollar, partly as a show of patriotism. The Mint Act of 1792 established the dollar as the official monetary unit of the U.S., and the first dollar coin was struck in 1794 (the federal government didn't print a paper dollar until 1862).

## "What are dollar bills made of?"

### Dr. T:

A secret formula that isn't really paper at all but a combination of cotton (75%) and linen (25%). That explains why the bills can survive even when kids forget that their allowance is in the pocket of their jeans and throw them into the washing machine. In fact, the Bureau of Engraving and Printing—the U.S. Treasury agency that prints money—washes bills over and over to test their durability.

# "Why is money green?"

### Dr. T:

To be honest, the Treasury Department doesn't really know for sure, but can make a good guess.

Back in 1861 the federal government authorized the issuance of its own paper money. But it immediately faced a threat from counterfeiters. What was needed was an ink with a colored tint that would make the bills difficult to duplicate by the black-and-white photography of the time. Such an ink was developed and patented by a man named Tracy R. Edson. The ink had a green tint, which came to be called patent green.

When U.S. currency was last redesigned and made smaller in 1929, the green tint was continued because ink of that color was available in large quantities, and the color was highly resistant to chemical and physical changes. Besides, by that time Americans had come to trust their money as a strong, stable currency.

# "Why are dollar bills called 'greenbacks'?"

### Dr. T:

That nickname comes from the color of the ink and the fact that it's used only on the *back* of paper money. Look closely and you'll see that the front of each bill is printed in black ink. The Treasury seal and serial numbers are green, but that's a different ink that's added later.

# "Who decided which portraits would be on each bill?"

## Dr. T:

The current portraits, along with the design on the back of each bill, were chosen by a committee appointed by the Secretary of the Treasury in 1929.

Here's the lineup: George Washington on the one-dollar bill, with the Great Seal of the United States on the back; Thomas Jefferson on the two-dollar bill, with a picture of the signing of the Declaration of Independence on the back; Abraham Lincoln on the five, with the Lincoln Memorial on the back; Alexander Hamilton (the first Secretary of the Treasury) on the ten, with the U.S. Treasury building on the back; Andrew Jackson on the twenty, with the White House on the back; Ulysses S. Grant on the fifty, with the U.S. Capitol on the back; and Benjamin Franklin on the hundred, with Independence Hall on the back.

Until the recent redesign of the hundred-dollar bill, the last significant change in the nation's paper money came in 1957, when the phrase "In God We Trust" was added.

## Money Talks

• • • • • • • • • • • • • • • • • • • • • • • •

In 1775, the Continental Congress authorized the issuance of currency to help pay for the Revolutionary War. Paul Revere, a silversmith by trade, actually made some of the first plates for this so-called "continental currency." But the bills quickly lost their value, giving rise to the expression "not worth a continental."

## "Can the government change the color of paper money or put a different picture on it?"

### Dr. T:

It could, but don't hold your breath waiting for a blue suede bill with Elvis on the front and Graceland on the back!

By law, the design features on U.S. currency must have historical and idealistic significance, may not include the likeness of a living person and may not have sectarian significance (favoring one religion over another). The government could theoretically replace the current portraits of deceased American statesmen. But tradition and psychology would probably outweigh any popular trend. Part of the reason the dollar has endured in value, both here and around the world, is that its design hasn't changed much over the years. The government would be reluctant to shake that confidence.

The same is true of the color of money. In recent years red and blue fibers have been embedded in U.S. currency, but that was intended as an anti-counterfeiting measure rather than a fashion statement. It's true that other countries print their currencies in different colors, but Americans tend to regard those as "funny money."

The U.S. government prints more currency than other countries, and U.S. dollars are more often the target of counterfeiters. The Treasury *wants* U.S. notes to be uniform in appearance so that people feel compelled to *look* at the bills when they're paying for something or getting change, instead of just reaching for a bill of a different color or size. By paying closer attention, you'll be more likely to spot something fishy.

*Part of the reason the dollar has endured in value, both here and around the world, is that its design hasn't changed much over the years.*

# "Why did the government redesign the $100 bill?"

### Dr. T:

The intent was more to foil counterfeiters than to make it look different. If you're lucky enough to have a $100 bill, the biggest change you'll notice in the new design is that the portrait of Benjamin Franklin is larger and slightly to the left of center. Over the next few years the $50, $20, $10 and $5 bills will be redesigned in a similar way (but the old bills will continue to be legal tender).

# "Has there ever been a woman's picture on American money?"

### Dr. T:

In addition to Susan B. Anthony, who appears on the dollar coins issued from 1979 to 1981, one other woman has appeared on U.S. currency—but not since 1896. Can you guess who that woman was?

a. Dolley Madison, President James Madison's wife, who saved valuable treasures when the British burned the White House during the War of 1812

b. Martha Washington, George's wife

c. Clara Barton, who gained fame as a nurse during the Civil War and eventually founded the American Red Cross

[And the answer is . . . Martha Washington!]

# "Who draws the pictures on U.S. money?"

### Dr. T:

U.S. currency is printed on presses using plates that are painstakingly engraved by hand by master engravers. There are less than twenty engravers in the country, and even in this age of computers they still work with hand tools similar to those used by Paul Revere. They're called letter engravers and picture engravers, and for each bill, one person does the signatures and all other letters, while another works on the pictures and decorative scrollwork.

## Small Change
• • • • • • • • • • • • • • • • • • • • • • • • • •

Before the federal government established an official U.S. currency, colonies, banks and even individuals issued their own money, which often wasn't worth the paper it was printed on. Even Benjamin Franklin got into the act, printing dollars on his own press for the colony of New Jersey. With typical Franklin bluntness, the motto on the bill read "Mind Your Business."

# "How much money does the government print every day?"

### Dr. T:

The Bureau of Engraving and Printing prints more than 35 million notes a day, with a face value of over $400 million, on its presses in Washington, D.C., and Fort Worth, Texas. Of the notes printed each year, 95% are used to replace bills already in circulation.

It costs a little less than four cents to print a bill of any denomination. Newly-printed bills break down approximately like this: ones, 45%; fives and tens, 12% each; twenties, 24%; fifties and hundreds, 4% each.

## "What's the biggest bill?"

**Dr. T:**

The $100 bill is the largest in circulation right now. The government used to issue notes in denominations of $500, $1,000, $5,000 and $10,000, but they were discontinued after 1969 because there was little demand for them. The largest bill ever printed had a face value of $100,000, but it was exchanged among banks and was never circulated to the public.

---

## Small Change

• • • • • • • • • • • • • • • • • • • • • • •

- Who was pictured on the $100,000 bill? (Woodrow Wilson.)

- You can fold a piece of paper money backward and forward about 4,000 times before it tears.

---

## "How long does paper money last?"

**Dr. T:**

That depends on the bill's denomination and how often it changes hands. For example, a $1 bill is handled most frequently and has the shortest average life—18 months. The average life span of other currency: $5 bill, two years; $10 bill, three years; $20 bill, four years; $50 bill, nine years; $100 bill, nine years.

## "What does the government do with worn-out money ?"

**Dr. T:**

It shreds the bills, then recycles or buries them. Each year the government destroys about $13 billion in worn-out currency.

# "What's that funny picture of a pyramid with an eye on top that's on the $1 bill?"

## Dr. T:

That's the reverse side of the Great Seal of the United States, which was adopted in 1782. At the base of the pyramid is the year 1776 in Roman numerals. The pyramid itself stands for permanence and strength, but it's unfinished, which signifies the future growth of the United States and the goal of perfection. The sunburst and the eye above the pyramid represent the overseeing eye of God.

The 13-letter motto, "Annuit Coeptis," means "He has favored our undertakings." Below the pyramid is the motto, "Novus Ordo Seclorum," which means "A new order of the ages" and stands for the new American era.

Even if they don't ask, you can impress your kids by telling them that the front of the Great Seal of the United States also appears on the back of the $1 bill. That's the picture of the American bald eagle behind the shield. The eagle holds in its right talon an olive branch that has 13 berries and 13 leaves. The olive branch stands for peace, and the number 13 always symbolizes the 13 original colonies. In its left talon, the eagle holds 13 arrows, representing war. The eagle's head is turned toward the olive branch, showing a desire for peace.

The top of the seal represents Congress, the head of the eagle the executive branch, and the nine tail feathers the judiciary branch of our government. The 13-letter motto, "E Pluribus Unum," on the ribbon held in the eagle's beak means "Out of Many, One."

## "What does the Treasurer of the United States do?"

### Dr. T:

The Treasurer of the United States, whose signature sharp-eyed kids will spot on the front of U.S. currency, is the Treasury Department official in charge of the U.S. Mint and the Bureau of Engraving and Printing. The Treasurer is not to be confused with his or her boss, the Secretary of the Treasury, whose signature also appears on U.S. currency.

## "If I accidentally tear a dollar bill and tape it back together, can I use it?"

### Dr. T:

Yes. You can use the bill even if you don't tape it back together as long as you clearly have more than half of the note. You can also take it to your local bank and exchange it for a new bill. That's also true for bills that are dirty, defaced, limp or just plain worn out.

It's illegal to intentionally deface a bill by doodling on it, for example. But you're unlikely to be prosecuted unless you make a habit of drawing moustaches on George Washington. In that case, your artistry may come to the attention of the Secret Service, the agency charged with tracking down counterfeiters and protecting the nation's currency.

# "If I only have a piece of a $1 bill, can I still use it?"

## Dr. T:

Not if it's less than half of the original note. In that case, your remnant is considered mutilated currency and isn't legal tender. If you want to exchange it for a new bill, you'll have to tell the Treasury Department how the money was damaged and provide evidence that the missing portion has been totally destroyed.

But if all you have is a small portion of a single bill, your chances of getting a replacement are slim. Each year the Treasury handles about 30,000 claims and redeems mutilated currency valued at over $30 million. But much of that is in the form of batches of bills that have been visibly damaged by fire, water, dirt, chemicals, explosives, rodents or insects. Nowadays, one of the biggest causes of mutilated money is microwave damage. When their money accidentally gets wet, people try to dry it in a microwave oven and end up turning their cash into ash!

All claims regarding mutilated currency are handled by the Department of the Treasury, Bureau of Engraving and Printing, OCS/BEPA, Room 344A, Washington, DC 20013.

## Money Talks

• • • • • • • • • • • • • • • • • • • • • • •

We've learned about the origin of the word "dollar," (see page 72) but the currencies of other nations often have interesting backgrounds. "Franc" comes from the Latin term "Francorum Rex," or "King of the Franks," an inscription that appeared on medieval French coins. Italy's "lira" comes from "libra," the Latin word for "pound." The "mark," used in Germany, means "to mark," or keep a tally. "Yen," the main unit of Japanese currency, is also the Japanese word for "circle." The theory is that money should "circulate."

# "How can I tell if a bill is counterfeit?"

### Dr. T:

Don't bother testing the ink to see if it smears. According to one bit of folk wisdom, a bill must be counterfeit if the ink rubs off. The truth is that genuine currency, when rubbed on paper, can leave ink smears, too. So the Secret Service doesn't recommend using the ink blot test to check out a suspect bill.

Instead, you should compare the suspect note with a genuine one of the same denomination and look for any differences in the characteristics of the paper or the quality of the printing. Genuine paper, for example, has tiny red and blue fibers embedded throughout. Counterfeiters often try to simulate those fibers by printing red and blue lines on their paper, but the lines are printed on the surface of the paper rather than embedded in it.

On a genuine bill, the overall printing is sharper and more distinct. Compare especially such features as the portraits, which should appear lifelike; the clarity of the sawtooth points of the Treasury seal; the serial numbers, which should be evenly spaced and printed in the same ink color as the Treasury seal; and the border, on which the fine lines should be clear and unbroken.

If you really believe you might have a counterfeit bill, the best thing to do is to put it in an envelope and take it to a bank or your local police department.

# "Can I see money actually being made?"

### Dr. T:

If you visit Washington, D.C., you can take a tour of the Bureau of Engraving and Printing. There's no charge for the tour, but in peak tourist seasons—spring vacation and during the summer—you need to pick up tour tickets in advance on the day of your visit (call 202-874-3188 for more information).

Two of the five U.S. Mints—in Denver and Philadelphia—are open for self-guided public tours. Contact the U.S. Mint Exhibits Office, 151 N. Independence Mall East, Philadelphia, PA, 19106; 215–597–7350 for more information.

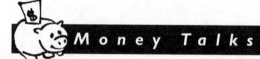

### Money Talks

Like the word "dollar" (see page 72), lots of our words for money and other financial terms have their roots in other languages.

- A **"doubloon,"** the English word for a Spanish gold coin, comes from the Spanish word for double, because a doubloon was worth twice as much as a smaller coin called a pistole.

- **"Picayune,"** a word we use to mean trifling, or of little value, comes from the French word for a small copper coin.

- **"Money"** itself comes from the Latin "moneta," meaning coin or mint. The Romans themselves "coined" that word from the temple of Juno Moneta, where Roman money was made. "Moneta" literally comes from the Latin word for warning; among other things, Juno, the queen of the gods, was also the goddess of warnings.

- **"Bank"** comes from the Italian word "banca," meaning bench. Hundreds of years ago, businessmen met outside on benches to borrow money or to entrust their savings to someone to invest on their behalf.

- **"Dime"** comes from the Latin word decimus, meaning "tenth." When Thomas Jefferson proposed this unit of currency, he called it the "disme," a French term, because the coin would be one-tenth the value and size of the dollar.

# "Grandma told me I could use my birthday money for 'mad money.' Does that mean I have to get mad before I spend it?"

### Dr. T:

Dr. T presumes most parents know that "mad money" is money you can blow on anything you want (even if they probably don't know where the expression originated). But parents shouldn't presume that their kids know what the phrase means—or, for that matter, that their kids understand any of the other money idioms and adages that litter our language.

We pay cash on the barrelhead, save for a rainy day, and put in our two cents. Some expressions are intuitive, some have historical roots in everyday experience, and some we owe to Benjamin Franklin, whose *Poor Richard's Almanac* was rich in financial wisdom—"A penny saved is a penny earned," "Penny wise and pound foolish."

But your children won't necessarily understand any of these expressions unless you explain them. Then, if you come up totally blank and can't think of any other response to their questions, at least they'll know what you're talking about.

By the way, the expression "mad money" came into common use in the 1920s. It referred to money a young woman carried with her on a date so that she could pay for busfare home if she got "mad" at her escort for inappropriate behavior!

# The Main Event: Allowances

**T**he number one topic of discussion between parents and children is allowances. First, the kids want to know if they can have one. No sooner do they get one, or so it seems, than they want an advance. And before you know it they're lobbying for a raise.

It isn't only parents and children who lock horns on this issue. Parents often disagree with each other about such things as how much to give and whether kids who get an allowance should be required to do chores as a quid pro quo.

No single allowance system will work for every family. But any system will work if you follow Dr. T's two basic rules for success. One: Don't start giving an allowance until your children are old enough to manage it. Two: Keep the system simple so that *you* can manage it.

# "Can I have an allowance?"

### You're tempted to say:

"You don't need one. We already give you all the money you need."

### Dr. T's Rx:

If you think that by denying your kids an allowance you'll be able to limit the amount of money they get their hands on, forget it. Studies show that kids who don't get allowances have access to about as much money as kids who do.

Since they're apparently going to get the money anyway, it's better to have them learn to manage it themselves than nickel and dime you to death. With an allowance, both of you will actually have more control over your children's finances—especially if you make it clear to the kids that the allowance isn't bonus cash, but will take the place of money you normally would have spent on such things as comic books, baseball cards, art supplies, hair bows, or other kid-related expenses.

You don't need to give an allowance until your children are at least 6 years old. (Remember that Dr. T's first rule for a foolproof allowance system is not to start too soon.) You don't want to rush things, and preschoolers generally don't understand the abstract idea of money anyway. Given a choice between a nickel and a dime, they'll almost invariably choose the nickel because it's bigger, even though the dime is worth more.

Once children start first grade they begin learning about money in school, so they'll know that if you

**Prices Then & Now**

| | | |
|---|---|---|
| 1960s | Baseball game (2 adults, 2 children) | $ 4.50 |
| 1970s | Baseball game (2 adults, 2 children) | $ 4.50 |
| Present | Baseball game (2 adults, 2 children) | $18.00 |

*General admission tickets at Dodger Stadium. To adjust earlier prices to account for the effects of inflation, multiply 1960s price by 5 and 1970s price by 3.*

*Prices courtesy of Team Marketing Report, Inc.*

give them a $1 bill each week, that's equivalent in value to ten dimes or four quarters. They'll also have some idea of how much their dollar will buy. If your child is 9, 10 or even older and you don't already give an allowance, it's not too late. Some parents have even started their kids on an allowance when they became teenagers as a rite of passage to becoming more grown up.

How much should you give? Dr. T thinks first-graders need at least $1 a week to do any serious spending or saving. As children get older you can adjust that amount upward depending on how much of their own expenses you expect them to cover. One family decided to put their 12-year-old son and 10-year-old daughter on monthly allowances of $50 and $40 respectively—which sounds like a lot until you consider that out of that money the kids were expected to buy birthday gifts for friends, pay for their own movie tickets and other entertainment, and still set aside money for savings and charity.

Giving kids a weekly allowance that's equal to their age is another option, but that tends to over-compensate younger children. And it's too rich for most parents, judging from the figures on average weekly allowances nationwide, based on a recent survey by Youth Monitor, a syndicated service of Nick-elodeon and Yankelovich Clancy Shulman. For 6- to 8-year-olds, the average is around $2; for 9- to 11-year-olds, about $4; for 12- and 13-year-olds, around $6; for 14- and 15-year-olds, about $10, and for 16- and 17-year-olds, around $11.

*Reprinted with special permission of King Features Syndicate*

# "Jessie's getting 'lowance, so why can't I?"

(Your 4-year-old immediately after you start giving your second-grader an allowance, as recommended in the previous question)

### You're tempted to say:

"Because you're too young."

### Dr. T's Rx:

That response isn't going to satisfy younger siblings, who catch on more quickly to everything (as you're already painfully aware).

Sibling rivalry is the one exception to Dr. T's rule about not giving preschoolers an allowance. If you're going to give your older child, say, $1 or $2 a week, go ahead and give younger brother or sister 50 cents. Chances are he or she won't understand how much that really is, so you might be able to get away with a quarter. The point is, give a token amount so he or she doesn't feel left out. And don't feel obliged to give anything unless your preschooler asks.

8-21

"Sorry, Billy, but we can't give you a raise that would exceed our allowance cap."

*Reprinted with special permission of King Features Syndicate*

# "How come Jessie gets a bigger 'lowance than I do?"

### You're tempted to say:
"Because Jessie's older."

### Dr. T's Rx:

Once the younger sibling wises up to the fact that two quarters is less than $2, it's probably time to rethink your system.

Assuming both children are of school age, Dr. T has a surefire way to avoid quibbling about differences in allowance. If the age differential between the children is two years or less, give them the same amount of money.

If the age gap is bigger—say, three or more years—to justify an allowance gap, don't be arbitrary about it. Spell out for your kids how the system works. For example, you might give a weekly allowance that's equal to half your children's age, so a 6-year-old would get $3 a week and a 10-year-old $5.

| Prices Then & Now | | |
|---|---|---|
| | **Roller skates** | **In-line skates** |
| 1960s | $ 5.99 | |
| 1970s | $ 6.99 | |
| 1980s | $11.00 | |
| Present | $25.00 | $ 79 (child) |
| | | $119–399 (adult) |

*To adjust earlier prices to account for the effects of inflation, multiply 1960s price by 5, 1970s price by 3 and 1980s price by 1.5.*

*Skates have shoes attached; prices courtesy of Roller Derby Inc. and Rollerblade Inc.*

That's slightly higher than the national averages, especially in the younger age groups, but it has the advantage of being easy to remember. Or you might set up your own allowance schedule, starting at $1 a week at age 6 and increasing by $1 a week on each birthday. When your kids are 13, say, you could switch to a monthly allowance as a reward for good money management skills. The point is, the kids know what to expect, so they don't need to ask.

# "Can I have a raise in my allowance?"

### *You're tempted to say:*
"You already get *twice* as much as I got when I was your age."

### *Dr. T's Rx:*
And when you were *their* age, things cost half as much! A kid's cost of living has increased considerably since you were a youth (just take a look at the "Prices Then & Now" boxes scattered throughout this book), and allowances should reflect that.

But there are limits. Tell your children you'd be willing to consider a raise if they can show, in writing, how they're spending their current allowance. *That* should nip frivolous requests in the bud. If your children rise to the occasion with a detailed accounting of income and outgo, it might be an a eye-opener for both of you. They may find that the reason they're flat broke by the end of the week is that they're pigging out on junk food—which suggests a need for better budgeting (not to mention better eating habits) rather than more money.

On the other hand, you may find that if you expect your children to pay for their own school lunches out of the money you give them, they don't have enough left over to fritter away on kid stuff. Any allowance system should adequately and accurately reflect your children's cost of living, based on what you expect them to pay for, and allow for a slush fund that they can spend as they wish. Giving your kids too little money is just as bad as giving them too much. In

## Money Talks

• • • • • • • • • • • • • • • • • • • • • • •

"Bread" and "dough" are both common slang terms for money, probably coming from the sentiment that money, like bread, is a necessity for survival. "Bread" first came into use in the 1930s, but was popularized by the Beat Generation of the late 1950s.

either case they aren't getting realistic experience in managing money. If you're cutting things too close, you may need to raise the allowance—or start paying for school lunches yourself.

One 11-year-old told Dr. T that when she wants a raise in her allowance, her parents make her come up with three good reasons why. Hint: "Because I need the money" doesn't count.

You can avoid this issue if you have an allowance system (like those described in the preceding question) with an annual adjustment date—the children's birthday, January 1 or the beginning of the school year. If your kids are on a work-for-pay system, do what your own boss would do and give them a periodic review in which you evaluate their performance and decide if the quality of their work, or an increase in their cost of living, merits a raise. One dad gives his two daughters a two-week allowance bonus every 13 weeks if they're doing a good job. He says it's cheaper than a raise, and the girls look forward to getting the lump sum.

"Cut off the allowance
and the body withers."

*Reprinted by permission of Andrew Toos*

# "How come you never have enough money to give me my allowance?"

### You're tempted to say:
"Because I forget."

### Dr. T's Rx:

Your honesty is refreshing, but your kids have a legitimate beef.

Start hoarding $1 bills, and get yourself on a regular schedule of paying your kids when you have the money on hand—on your own payday, when you're paying the household bills, or on Sunday night when you're parceling out cash for the week ahead (giving your kids their allowance on Sunday instead of Friday will also keep them from blowing it all over the weekend).

You might even want to assess yourself a penalty—

## A Look at Allowance Kits

Despite the best of intentions, families sometimes have a tough time coming up with and sticking to an allowance system that works. A number of allowance kits on the market try to provide the discipline and follow-through you need, either by reminding you to pay up or reminding your kids what they're supposed to do with their money once they get it.

Each system is based on its own philosophy of how much allowance kids should get, how it should be divvied up and how closely it should be tied to chores. So choose one that's in sync with your own philosophy (for Dr. T's thoughts on those questions, see the responses in this chapter).

- **The Allowance Kit** (800–367–2548; $39.95 plus $6.95 shipping) comes with an audiocassette, a slick handbook and stickers kids can use to decorate the heart of the kit—a three-part plastic bank with one section for spending and giving, one for saving, and one for investing. The investment compartment is the largest, on the theory that money here won't be touched for a long time. The kit also has lists for tracking chores, but the allowance isn't directly tied to chores.

say 50 cents or $1, depending on how much the children get—when you're late. (This can work both ways: You can assess your kids a penalty—or even confiscate the cash—if they habitually forget to put their money away and leave it on the kitchen counter).

Some families have come up with creative and inexpensive solutions. One mom took scrap paper and made her two sons "coupon books," each with 52 dated coupons, one for every week of the year. Each coupon was good for a weekly allowance payment, and Mom agreed to pay the kids on demand for each coupon they turned in, even if they turned in more than one at a time. But each coupon could be used only once.

A variation on this for older children is to credit their allowance account (at the Bank of Mom and Dad) with a certain amount per month, and use old check registers to keep a running tally as the kids draw down the balance by making withdrawals. One dad formalized his version of this system into a kit (see the accompanying box).

- **ParentBanc** (800–483–3883; $15.95 plus $3 for shipping) is geared to helping forgetful parents, who don't actually have to come up with any cash at allowance time. Instead, kids get their own checkbook in which they credit deposits (allowance, gifts, earnings), and then write checks when they want to make withdrawals (payable by mom and dad). It's up to the kids to decide how much to save or spend, as long as they keep the register up to date.

- **Monthly Money** (800–547–4848; $19.95 plus $5 shipping) pays kids as young as age 6 a monthly allowance, which is expected to cover lots of expenses in a child's budget, including clothing (except for certain basics and special dress clothes) and gifts for family members. The kit itself includes a vinyl money folder with sections for each line item in the budget. Payment isn't tied directly to chores, but kids can be fined if they don't do agreed-upon work around the house.

## "Why do I have to use my own money to pay for the movies?"

### You're tempted to say:
"Because I buy you plenty of other things."

### Dr. T's Rx:
That's a good start, but be more specific by making clear to your kids what they'll have to buy with their own money. An allowance shouldn't be extra cash on top of everything else you already give your children. In exchange, they should have to take over certain bills you're footing now.

How do you decide what expenses your kids should cover? It doesn't matter how much or how little they have to pay for as long as they have to pay for something. Their responsibilities should depend on their age and your expectations.

| Prices Then & Now | | |
|---|---|---|
| 1960s | box of 64 Crayola™ crayons | $1.00 |
| 1970s | box of 64 Crayola™ crayons | $1.69 |
| Present | box of 64 Crayola™ crayons | $5.42 |

*To adjust earlier prices to account for the effects of inflation, multiply 1960s price by 5 and 1970s price by 3.*

*Prices courtesy of Binney & Smith, Inc.*

Some parents give their children a relatively small allowance and consider it mad money. Others hand out a bigger amount, out of which older kids are expected to pay for such basics as school lunches or clothing. Either system can work if you follow a few general rules:

**Start small,** especially with younger children. Put them in charge of the single thing they most like to spend your money on, whether it's comic books, video arcade games, or popcorn at the movies.

One mother, who is an artist, often takes her 7-year-old daughter, Roxanne, to museums, where the child loves to buy trinkets from the gift shop—with her mother's money. Mom finally told Roxanne that she would have to use her own allowance to buy souvenirs. As if by magic, Roxanne became more conscientious about bringing money with her—and the price of the souvenirs she purchased dropped drastically.

**Anticipate conflicts.** Suppose you expect your kids to pay for their own tickets when they go to the movies with friends. Then suppose your whole family goes to see a movie as a holiday treat. Who pays? One mom and dad decreed that on family outings parents would pay for the tickets—but the kids would have to buy their own popcorn.

In another case, a mother wanted to encourage her 9-year-old to read without going broke buying books for him. She agreed to pay for up to $5 worth of books when Sam brought home the monthly order form from his school book club. Above that, he was on his own.

**Adopt a system you feel comfortable with.** As your kids get older, you may or may not want them in charge of paying for school lunches (see chapter 2) or clothes (see the question on page 108). Parents often disagree about what's appropriate.

Whatever you decide, be sensible. If you expect your junior high student to manage his lunch money, build extra cash for that purpose into his allowance. High school students can get a separate clothing allowance equal to what you'd spend each season. If they want a bigger wardrobe, it should come out of their discretionary spending.

HOW TO TELL YOUR CHILD'S ALLOWANCE IS TOO HIGH...

YES, MY CLIENT IS AWARE OF HOW HARD HIS MOTHER WORKED TO MAKE SCALLOPED POTATOES, BUT WE STILL FIND THEM ICKY, SO I'M ADVISING HIM TO HOLD OUT FOR FRENCH FRIES

8-28

© 1995, Washington Post Writers Group. Reprinted with permission.

# "How much will you give me if I make my bed every day?"

### You're tempted to say:

"You don't see me getting paid for working around the house, do you?"

### Dr. T's Rx:

If you make it sound as though you suffer chores grudgingly, and think yourself ill-used for having to do them, your children can't help but think the same.

Next time your kids ask, tell them what Dr. T tells her children—that if they make their beds you'll give them your undying love and affection. You'll ease the tension with a little humor and put a more positive spin on household tasks—which, you can remind your kids, everyone in the family (including you) pitches in to do without pay.

Don't tie your kids' entire allowance to the chores they do. Keeping the allowance separate makes things easier on you—remember Dr. T's second rule for a foolproof allowance system—because it's less labor-intensive for parents. You don't have to set up a pay schedule and monitor work performed. You also avoid turning your kids into little mercenaries, who may someday decide that since they don't

*Reprinted with special permission of King Features Syndicate*

need the money they won't do the chores—or who, when asked to help unload groceries from the car, reply, "How much is it worth to you?"

An allowance isn't a giveaway as long as you exact certain financial responsibilities from your children in return for the money—requiring them to pay for their own movie tickets, video games, hobby items or other expenses appropriate to their age.

Kids do need to learn about working for pay, of course, but you can get that lesson across by paying for extra jobs beyond regular household duties.

At this point, you parents probably have a question of your own: If I don't pay them, how am I going to get them to do the chores? You might let them choose what work they'll be responsible for. That should cut down on their complaints, and increase their job satisfaction. You could be creative in your definition of what constitutes a chore. Planning and cooking a meal once a week is probably a bigger help to you—and more fun for them—than washing dishes.

Or you could simply try asking. Parents often brace for a confrontation with their kids, but younger children especially are often happy to cooperate if you simply ask in a matter-of-fact way. One man recalls his mother's technique: "She'd say, 'Can you please do me a favor?' and how could I say no? It still works today, and I'm 40 years old."

*Kids do need to learn about working for pay, of course, but you can get that lesson across by paying for extra jobs beyond regular household duties.*

*What counts isn't the size of the weekly dole, but the experience kids get with making it last.*

# "How come my friend Christopher's allowance is bigger than mine?"

## You're tempted to say:
"Because Christopher's parents have more money than we do."

## Dr. T's Rx:
Your income shouldn't be the only factor, or even the main one, that determines your children's allowance.

Tell your kids up front that their allowance will be based on three things: how much you can afford to give, what you expect them to pay for, and how much money you think they can comfortably handle. If they bring up the subject again, you have a ready-made reply to rattle off.

In asking this question, your kids may be dancing around what's really on their mind. They may be fishing for a raise in their allowance (see the question earlier in this chapter). Or they may be trying to keep up with the Jones kids (see Chapter 3).

If you really can't afford to come up with more money, that can work to your advantage. What counts isn't the size of the weekly dole, but the experience kids get with making it last. If you have to limit your kids' income because your own is stretched, that's a lesson in real-world economics, and your kids will be better off for learning it. With more money to spare, Christopher's parents will have a *tougher* time teaching him the value of a dollar.

## "Can I have an advance on my allowance?"

### You're tempted to say:

"Didn't I just give you an advance on your allowance?"

### Dr. T's Rx:

Don't count on getting a straight answer if you ask a question like this. Your kids are fervently hoping you'll forget about any money they owe you. You need to keep meticulous records, or have a steel-trap memory, to keep from being rolled.

That's why it's best to just say "no advances." Besides, an allowance is supposed to help kids learn about deferred gratification. If you expect your children to save their own money to buy compact discs, it's self-defeating to advance a couple of weeks worth of allowance so they can buy the hottest release today.

That being said, Dr. T knows there will be times when some loan seems reasonable—especially if your kids don't ask too often and are generally responsible money managers. Rather than giving them an advance, however, simplify your bookkeeping by lending them the money for a specific purpose and a specific payback period. When one young man asked to borrow $250 from his parents to buy a bicycle, he also presented them with a list of extra chores and special jobs he could do to earn money to pay off the loan, and even offered to pay $50 interest. He earned $100 by painting his grandmother's porch, and made all the money over the course of one summer.

What you're trying to avoid is a permanent pattern of borrowing money that keeps your kids chronically in debt, and leaves you confused about exactly how much they owe.

*Rather than giving them an advance, however, simplify your bookkeeping by lending them the money for a specific purpose and a specific payback period.*

# "Will you buy me that [fill in the blank] if I pay you back when we get home?"

### You're tempted to say:

"You should have brought money with you."

### Dr. T's Rx:

Now you're talking. This kind of short-term loan carries the same risks as an advance against allowance. Your kids should be learning how to plan ahead and bring their own money.

# "Can I have $5 to go to the movies?"

### You're tempted to say:

"Isn't movie money supposed to come out of your allowance?"

### Dr. T's Rx:

Are you asking or telling? Telling, Dr. T hopes. You're the one who set up the system, so you ought to know what it's supposed to cover. If movie admissions are your children's responsibility, don't make it sound as if there's some doubt about that—and some chance of getting extra money. Note: This is a variation of the preceding two questions, only in this case your kids are trying to get the money as a freebie so they don't have to pay it back at all.

# "Will you still give me my allowance while we're on vacation?"

### You're tempted to say:

"No, because you won't need it then."

### Dr. T's Rx:

On the contrary, vacations give kids a lot more opportunity to spend money, and there's no reason why it should all come out of your pocket.

Not only should you continue your children's allowance while you're away, you should even consider giving it to them before you leave. That way they'll have their own money to spend on souvenirs or other extras that you're not willing to buy.

Work out in advance who's going to pay for what, so that you can avoid having to make ad hoc decisions en route. Before embarking on a 35-state road trip with their two children, ages 9 and 7, one mom and dad told the kids they'd pay for patches and postcards at stops along the way. The kids had to buy other souvenirs with their special vacation allowance of $1 per day. Another family includes snacks and desserts in their children's travel budget. "We will buy no snacks or desserts unless it is our choice, not because someone has asked," says Mom. "It is amazing how this system has virtually eliminated whining for this or that souvenir or food item."

## Money Talks

• • • • • • • • • • • • • • • • • • • • • •

You'll sometimes hear money referred to as "scratch," which started in the 1920s. It probably comes from the scratching around a chicken does to find food. Sometimes we've got to scratch around to find money!

# "Can I have extra money to spend on holiday presents?"

### You're tempted to say:

"Wouldn't we all like extra money to spend during the holidays?"

### Dr. T's Rx:

In fact, some of us *do* get a bonus at this time of year if business is good and we've done our job well. If you think your children have done a good job of managing their money or keeping up with their chores, Dr. T can justify a spontaneous something extra in their pre-Christmas stocking.

But don't make it merely a handout. Even children realize that buying a present for Mom or Dad isn't the same if Mom or Dad has to put up the cash for the gift. As an alternative to giving a bonus, encourage your kids to do extra chores to earn money or to tap their piggy banks (buying gifts is an appropriate reason to dip into savings, in Dr. T's opinion).

Emphasize to your children that presents don't have to cost a lot. If you'd rather not give them money, offer advice instead:

- **Make a list.** What's good for Santa is even better for kids. Writing things down helps them get organized

## Prices Then & Now

| | | |
|---|---|---|
| 1970 | Basic cable (2-14 channels) | $ 5.50 per month |
| 1980 | Basic cable (19-64 channels) | $ 7.00 per month |
| 1990 | Basic cable (65-94 channels) | $ 15.78 per month |
| Present | Basic cable (102 channels) | $ 21.62 per month |

*To adjust earlier prices to account for the effects of inflation, multiply 1970 price by 4, 1980 price by 1.75 and the 1990 price by 1.15.*

*Prices courtesy of Manhattan Cable; number of channels courtesy of National Cable Television Association.*

ahead of time, keep focused once they get to the store and stay within their budget.

- **Check it twice.** Take the kids on a pre-shopping trip without cash in hand. Children tend to spend everything they have on the first thing they see. Scouting the stores in advance will help them find things they like and can afford, as well as learn how to tell the difference between something that's a bargain and something that's merely cheap.

- **Don't throw your catalogs away.** Sit down with your kids and look through them. They're a great tool not only for finding gift ideas but also for giving your children a sense of how much things cost.

- **Make a push for kid-made gifts.** Parents, grandparents and even siblings can be suckers for cards, decorations or crafts that are handmade, or even computer-generated.

- **Next year, start a holiday club.** If the children begin putting aside gift money around Labor Day, they should have a tidy little fund to help them buy presents in December.

**"I mean it, young lady. Until you see fit to clean this room, your allowance will be held in escrow!"**

*Gerberg/Cartoonists & Writers Syndicate*

## Where It Goes

An allowance shouldn't be free money on top of everything else you buy your kids. In exchange for the money, you can expect them to take on the responsibility of paying for certain things that you've bought in the past. Each family will have different expectations, depending on how big the allowance is and what your kids like to spend money on.

Your children are likely to get income from other sources as well, especially as they get older—gifts, extra chores they do around the house, odd jobs for neighbors, a part-time job, maybe even their own business—and their list of responsibilities will expand. You're the parent, and it's appropriate for you to set some rules about how the kids' money is spent or saved—as long as you leave them some money to burn and the freedom to burn it.

Here's how income and outgo might expand to fit kids of varying ages:

### 6-YEAR-OLD
**Income**

| | |
|---|---|
| Allowance | $ _____ |
| Gifts | _____ |
| Extra chores | _____ |
| **Total income** | $ _____ |

**Expenses**

| | |
|---|---|
| Saving | $ _____ |
| Giving | _____ |
| Loans to be repaid | _____ |
| Books | _____ |
| Arcade games | _____ |
| Snacks | _____ |
| Toys | _____ |
| Hobbies or collectibles | _____ |
| Gifts for family members | _____ |
| Extras/Mad money | _____ |
| **Total expenses** | $ _____ |

### 12-YEAR-OLD

**Income**

Allowance   $ _____

Gifts _____

Extra chores _____

Odd jobs for neighbors _____

Own business _____

**Total income**   $ _____

**Expenses**

Saving   $ _____

Giving _____

Loans to be repaid _____

Books _____

Snacks _____

Hobbies or collectibles _____

Gifts for family members
and friends _____

School supplies _____

Movie tickets _____

CDs _____

Video game rentals _____

Electronic stuff _____

School lunches _____

Bus fare or other
public transportation _____

Extras/Mad money _____

**Total Expenses**   $ _____

### 16-YEAR-OLD

**Income**

Allowance   $ _____

Clothing allowance _____

Gifts _____

Extra chores _____

Odd jobs _____

Own business _____

Part-time job _____

**Total income**   $ _____

**Expenses**

Saving   $ _____

College saving _____

Giving _____

Loans to be repaid _____

Books _____

Snacks _____

Hobbies or collectibles _____

Gifts for friends and
family members _____

School supplies _____

Movies and other
entertainment _____

CDs _____

Video rentals _____

Electronic stuff _____

School lunches _____

Bus fare or other
public transportation _____

Field trips _____

Concert tickets _____

Clothing _____

Gasoline _____

Car-related expenses _____

Car insurance _____

**Total expenses**   $ _____

# "Why do I have to save part of my allowance?"

### You're tempted to say:
"I don't want you to spend it all."

### Dr. T's Rx:
Spending all their money sounds like fun; saving it sounds like a drag. If you really want your children to appreciate the value of thrift, you'll have to make it sound more attractive. Appeal to their acquisitive instincts. Tell them you're making them save *small* amounts of money now so they can afford to buy something *really big* later.

| Prices Then & Now | | |
|---|---|---|
| 1981 | Entry-level computer | $2,665 |
| 1987 | Entry-level computer | $1,695 |
| Present | Entry-level computer | $1,900 |

*To adjust earlier prices to account for the effects of inflation, multiply 1981 price by 1.6 and the 1987 price by 1.3.*

*Prices courtesy of IBM. Personal computers have changed so radically since their introduction in the early '80s that comparisons are extremely tenuous. For example, the 1981 model cited here had 1 megabyte of storage, while the current model boasts 1 gigabyte.*

It's okay for kids to dip into savings to buy something they want. In fact, having a goal is what gives kids (or adults, for that matter) the incentive to keep going. But make the goal appropriate to your child's age. It's better for a 6-year-old to save for new crayons than for college. Once children get into the habit of saving, their goals can grow with them (see Chapter 8 for more about saving).

Some kids are natural squirrelers, who won't need much more encouragement from you than a pat on the back. Some are natural spenders, who will need a push in the right direction. It's fine for you to require them to save part of their allowance. But remember Dr. T's second rule for a successful allowance: Keep it simple. Putting aside a flat 10% or 25% is easier than parceling savings into different pots. Save that for when your children are old enough to do their own bookkeeping.

## "It's my money, so why can't I spend it the way I want?"

### You're tempted to say:

"Because you're living in my house, and I make the rules."

### Dr. T's Rx:

Sometimes even Dr. T is hard-pressed to improve on an old cliché.

Your gut reaction is more on target than perhaps you and your children realize. As long as you're supporting your children, you're entitled to at least a portion of their income. Few parents would be inclined to exercise that right. But if you're trying to teach financial values, it's appropriate for you to have some say about how your kids manage their money. That's true even for teenagers—especially for teenagers, who may be earning real money and shouldn't get the idea that all income is discretionary.

You can't have total control over your children's money because that would defeat the whole purpose of an allowance. But if you don't want your 8-year-old to buy a skateboard with his own money because you think it's too dangerous, put your foot down. If you don't want your 15-year-old to have a television in her own room because it would be a distraction from studies, pull the plug.

The sooner your children become accustomed to your household's rules about money, the less inclined they'll be to balk later on.

*If you're trying to teach financial values, it's appropriate for you to have some say about how your kids manage their money.*

# "Can I have a clothing allowance?"

(Asked by your 15-year-old son)

### You're tempted to say:

"I shudder to think what you'd come home with."

### Dr. T's Rx:

Dr. T shudders in sympathy. But if there's one thing worse than a 15-year-old on the loose at the mall with a clothing allowance, it's an 18-year-old on the loose with a credit card of his own. An allowance at least limits your losses.

Tell your son you'll consider a clothing allowance if he earns the privilege by passing a shopper's-ed course of your own creation.

"May I have $50 in travelers checks?"

*Farris/Cartoonists & Writers Syndicate*

Lesson one is taking inventory of every article of clothing he owns, including underwear, socks and pajamas.

Lesson two is having him make a list of all the things he needs, as well as things he wants. Then tell him what you think is a reasonable allowance—the amount you'd typically spend on his clothes each season, for example.

With the help of catalogs, lesson three is letting him practice matching a new wardrobe with the available funds. With luck, he'll learn that 1) he can't possibly afford five silk shirts, or 2) he'll have to shop in cheaper catalogs—both valuable lessons.

Now he's ready for a dress rehearsal by going with you on a shopping trip. To make the task less overwhelming, limit your itinerary to, say, three stores. Add your own commentary along the way: How to spot a bargain at sales or off-price stores; how to choose clothes that won't fall apart in the wash; how to choose clothes that are stylish but not faddish, so they'll last more than one season. Tell him what, if anything, you won't finance.

The final exam is an excursion on his own. Don't grade him on his choice of styles and colors—you'll have to live with those, within the limits you've set—but on how well he manages his money. It's okay to splurge on a silk shirt as long as he finds a great deal on jeans or buys his quota of socks. If he shops smart, reward him with a seasonal allowance.

You can always tailor a clothing allowance to your own situation. Lest kids skimp on undies or go overboard on a leather jacket, some parents continue to buy the basics, such as underwear and coats, or dispense money in more manageable monthly chunks.

The idea is to teach your kids how to function in the marketplace, so that when they're legally able to shop with their own credit cards they'll show both good sense and good taste.

**CHAPTER**

**8**

# Banks: Piggies to ATMs

**P**icture the scene: You're in the car with the kids running your usual weekend errands when your seven-year-old pipes up from the back seat, "Let's go to McDonald's for lunch." "I don't have money for that today," you reply. "Why don't you just go to the bank machine and get some?" asks your little darling

Nothing drives parents crazier than their kids' innocent assumption that money materializes out of nowhere. But look at it from your kids' point of view. They've seen you withdraw cash from an ATM countless times; they've probably even pushed the buttons themselves. They see you buy things without using money at all, simply by writing your name on a check or handing over a piece of plastic. Why *shouldn't* they think that money is printed on tiny presses hidden inside ATMs—or, nowadays, materializes out of hyperspace?

Not only do kids have misconceptions about how to get money out of a bank, but they're also not always clear about what happens to their money when they put it in. Banks, sometimes even piggy banks, seem to swallow up cash and never spit it out. Kids need you to spell out where money comes from, and where it goes.

# "I have $35 in my piggy bank. Can I spend it on a building set?"

### You're tempted to say:

"It took you months to save that money, and now you want to blow it all on one overpriced toy?"

### Dr. T's Rx:

Go ahead, let them blow it. If your kids have exercised the self-discipline to save the money in the first place, they deserve a reward.

Parents should certainly retain some veto power over how children spend their own money. You may not want them to have inline skates, for example, because you think they're too dangerous, or a video game system because you do'n't want them to be parked in front of the TV all day.

But price alone shouldn't be the deciding factor. Even if the coveted item is expensive relative to your kids' allowance, let them splurge as long as the purchase is otherwise suitable. Gazing upon the vast emptiness in their piggy bank will be a lesson in itself.

*Reprinted with special permission of King Features Syndicate*

# "Why don't you just go to the bank machine and get some money?"

### You're tempted to say:
"Do you think money grows on trees?"

### Dr. T's Rx:

A tree that sprouts greenbacks. A parent who's "made of money." The old images are colorful, but not very useful. Your children already think cash pops out of bank machines, and now you've really confused them.

Tell them instead that bank machines don't actually print money (which is what your kids may think). Explain that you get paid for working at your job and that you deposit your paycheck into your bank account for safekeeping. When you get money from the bank machine you're actually taking money out of your own account. When the account is empty, it's empty.

You'd be surprised at how many children of all ages (and plenty of adults, too) don't make that connection. Making it for them will only take a minute or two, and could head off some big problems later on—as in the unusual but true case of the 13-year-old who used his parents' bank card to withdraw $1,500 from their account before they finally caught on, when their checks starting bouncing. The boy had withdrawn the money in small increments—nothing bigger than $100—and spent most of it treating his buddies to video games and pizza.

---

## Money Talks

● ● ● ● ● ● ● ● ● ● ● ● ● ● ● ● ● ● ● ● ● ● ●

"Two bits, four bits, six bits, a dollar..."

A Spanish "real" or "bit" was worth 12½ cents, or ⅛ of a Spanish "peso." So, "two bits," or 25 cents, came to stand for our quarter. In addition, "Pieces of Eight," made famous by parrots in pirate stories, referred to the Spanish peso (worth eight "reals"). Not only was it marked with the number 8, but it could also be broken into eight pieces, which brings us right back to bits.

---

The boy's parents blamed the incident partly on youthful thoughtlessness and partly on themselves for never explaining the direct link between an ATM and their checking account. By age 13 their son might have been expected to figure that out for himself. But he didn't–or else convinced himself that he'd never get caught.

When he was, his parents didn't throttle him (although they were sorely tempted). But they did exact a stiff penalty: He had to get a job and repay the $1,500, along with an additional $1,500 (which his parents, without his knowledge, used to fund a savings account for him). He was also grounded for several months, during which he had plenty of time to sit down with his folks and watch them pay the household bills.

In this case, the parents couldn't claim that the ATM transactions weren't authorized because they had let their son see their personal identification number. But even if their son had gotten their PIN without their knowledge, they would have been in a bind. They could have limited their liability by claiming the card had been stolen, but they would have had to be willing to let the bank prosecute their son.

**"Why do you hafta go to work Daddy, if you can get money here?"**

*Reprinted with special permission of King Features Syndicate*

# "How does a bank machine work?"

### You're tempted to say:
"Beats me."

### Dr. T's Rx:
You don't have to be a technological wizard to take a stab at this one, even if it's only to assure your child there isn't a person inside the machine dealing out $10 bills. Here's all you need to know:

An ATM is like a computerized teller. You talk to the computer with your bank card, which tells the machine who you are. The machine then calls your bank to find out if you have enough money in your account to cover the amount of cash you're requesting. If so, the machine gives you the cash. If not, you're out of luck.

How does the cash actually get into the machine? It's loaded there by bank employees or outside security firms. Sometimes machines are "cashed up" several times a day because banks don't like to load them with large amounts. But over a long holiday weekend, for example, machines will hold more cash than normal.

---

## Small Change
• • • • • • • • • • • • • • • • • • • • • • • •

The average ATM withdrawal is $55, but many machines don't dispense $5 bills. The $20 bill is by far the most common. The greater the variety of bills handled by an ATM, the more complex and expensive the machine has to be. Some sophisticated ATMs can even cash your check to the penny.

# "Can I open my own bank account?"

### You're tempted to say:
"Aren't you a little young?"

### Dr. T's Rx:

If your children are old enough to ask this question they're probably old enough to have an account. Banks will often let kids open a savings account as soon as they're able to sign their own name. As long as the kids are minors, however, you'll probably have to co-sign the account as custodian.

If your kids raise the subject of a bank account on their own, seize the moment before their interest fades. Aside from your own inertia (it can be a pain in the neck to take your kids to the bank on a Saturday morning when you're used to transacting your own business via ATMs at odd hours), the biggest stumbling block isn't how old your children are but how much money they have. Many banks impose minimum balance requirements or levy service charges that can eat away at small accounts, so you should always ask about special deals on accounts for kids. And check out credit unions if you're eligible to join any.

Dr. T's rule of thumb is that once your children have more than $100 socked away in their sock drawer, it's time to look into a real bank account. But it's okay to keep about $50 in the drawer; your kids won't have an ATM card to get access to ready cash.

For a really warm welcome, try a bank that caters to kids—Young Americans Bank (311 Steele St., Denver, CO 80206; 303–321–2265), where the average savings depositor is 9 years old and has a balance of about $260. The bank has mail-in customers from all 50 states.

*Dr. T's rule of thumb is that once your children have more than $100 socked away in their sock drawer, it's time to look into a real bank account.*

*Even kids who have the money and the savvy to open an account of their own aren't always clear on what happens to their money once it goes in.*

# "If I put my $20 bill into the bank, will I be able to get it out again?"

### You're tempted to say:

"Of course you will."

### Dr. T's Rx:

Before you're too quick to answer, make sure you understand the question, which may in fact be a two-parter: First, will I be able to get my $20 back, and second, will I be able to get the *same* $20 back. The answers, of course, are "yes" and "no," which may be obvious to you but not to your children.

Even kids who have the money and the savvy to open an account of their own aren't always clear on what happens to their money once it goes in. They're shocked to find that their crumpled bills and painstakingly rolled coins aren't being kept on a shelf for them until they want the money back.

A brief explanation of how a bank works may be in order. Tell your kids that the bank uses their money to make loans to other people, but that they can always withdraw an amount equal to their account balance. In return for letting the bank use their money, the bank will pay them interest, which is figured as a percentage of their balance and added to their account periodically. They'll most likely get a regular statement in the mail that shows their balance and the interest earned.

**Note:** When you open an account with your kids, be sure to ask whether they can make withdrawals on their own or will need your signature to take money out.

# "How could my checking account be empty? I still have lots of checks left."

***You're tempted to say:***
"That's a joke, right?"

### Dr. T's Rx:

It's not a joke. It certainly wasn't funny to one woman who told Dr. T that when she was in college, she walked into a bank, only to get cold feet because she didn't know the difference between checking and savings accounts. She left without opening either. And it wasn't funny to the panicked student who showed a professor what he feared were bounced checks, but were really *cleared* checks.

Giving young kids a simple explanation of how checking accounts work can avoid big problems later. Dr. T witnessed an exchange between a mother and her 8-year-old, who was begging her mom to register her for gymnastics. Mom explained that she wouldn't have enough money until Friday. "You can write a check," said the child. "It wouldn't matter," Mom replied. "There won't be any money in the account until your dad and I get paid on Friday." The child accepted this explanation without a fuss.

Lesson one for kids, which they often pick up on their own, is that a check is a substitute for cash. Lesson two, which doesn't always occur to them, is where the money ultimately comes from to make good on the check. Lesson three is watching you write checks and subtract their value from your bank account. If they've absorbed that by the time they leave home at 18, they may run out of checks, but they're less likely to run out of cash.

*Saving money successfully requires a system, a goal, or a reward, and sometimes a combination of all three.*

## 66How come I can't seem to save money?99

### You're tempted to say:
"Because you're always spending it."

### Dr. T's Rx:
When children come to you with this question, they *know* they're spending too much money. Instead of pointing out the obvious, you should be pleased that they've sought your help and try to come up with a constructive solution.

Opening a bank savings account isn't necessarily the answer—yet. Thrift should begin at home, one step at a time. Saving money successfully requires a system, a goal, or a reward, and sometimes a combination of all three.

- **Have your kids divvy up their allowance** among different envelopes for spending and saving. When the spending envelope is empty, that's it until the next allowance day.

- **Hang on to a portion of their allowance** if you think they can't be trusted not to raid the savings envelope.

- **Encourage them to save their money to buy something specific,** and suitable for their age. For younger children it might be an action figure; for older kids, a CD. For kids under the age of 12 or 13, "saving for college" is often too fuzzy a goal and too far in the future. They need a more tangible reward for their efforts. But teenagers should certainly be saving for their education.

- **Offer to match whatever they put aside.** Whether you match their savings dollar for dollar or even 50 cents on the dollar, your contribution will still give your kids a powerful incentive. When one 7-year-old announced her intention to save $150 to buy a lap-

top computer for kids, her parents figured her interest and her patience would flag long before she
reached such a lofty goal. To make the amount
seem more attainable, they broke it into smaller
chunks, offering to contribute $1 for every $10 she
saved. She stuck it out and got the computer, but
even if she had quit at $90 it would have been a
worthwhile effort.

- **Suggest that they not take money with them when
  they hang out with their friends,** or take exactly
  what they need to play two video games and buy a
  soft drink. What they don't have they won't spend.

- **Make a deal.** One eight-year-old who constantly
  dipped into her savings to buy an ever-growing pile
  of Pogs negotiated with her parents for one more
  $5 purchase, and then agreed to add to her collec-
  tion by trading with friends. Another over-eager
  collector set a monthly limit of $10 to be spent on
  sports cards.

## Prices Then & Now

| | | |
|---|---|---|
| 1960s | Portable tape recorder/player | $40– $80 |
| 1970s | Portable tape recorder/player | $50–$100 |
| 1980s | "Walkman" | $75–$130 |
| Present | Portable compact disc player | $85–$180 |

*To adjust earlier prices to account for the effects of inflation, multiply the 1960s price by 5, the 1970s price by 3, and the 1980s price by 1.5.*

**CHAPTER**

**9**

# To Market, To Market

**D**on't make the mistake of thinking that investing in the stock market is for adults only, sort of like an R-rated movie. On the contrary, it's more like PG-13. Children that age, or even younger, are able to understand how the market works, and, with a little parental guidance, become successful investors.

Kids who own stock are in the minority among children, but they're a vocal and savvy group. Dr. T has met sixth-graders who triumphed in the Stock Market Game, a 10-week project in which teams of students vie to turn $100,000 in play money into a winning portfolio. She has met a 12-year-old who publishes his own investment newsletter—and runs his father's individual retirement account.

In Dr. T's experience, the children most likely to take an interest in stocks fall into three categories:

- Kids who already have their own savings accounts and start to notice that at today's rates their money isn't growing very fast.

- Kids whose grandparents, parents, or friends invest in the stock market.

- Entrepreneurial kids who have earned several hundred dollars or more at a job or business and have bigger plans for their money than a bank account.

Although they have a nodding acquaintance with Wall Street, children don't always understand its twists and turns—nor, if truth be told, do many adults. Dr. T is bombarded with requests from parents and grandparents for material specially written to help children get started in the stock market.

The first thing parents and kids should understand is the principle of a market: Sellers ask a high price for their wares, buyers bid lower, and they reach an agreement somewhere in the middle. And that's it. No matter how complex they sound, no matter how sophisticated their computers, all markets are fundamentally the same, whether you're buying and selling stocks, baseball cards or foreign currency. And the goal of an investor is always the same, too: Buy low, sell high.

With that bit of knowledge in hand, you're ready to begin. If you have any budding investors around the house, hand them this book (after you've finished, of course). The following pages are written for all would-be Wall Street tycoons.

"Do you want to put it all into the same stock?"

*Toos/Cartoonists & Writers Syndicate*

# "If I have a share of stock, does that mean I have to share it with someone?"

## Dr. T:

*Sometimes even a profitable company doesn't pay dividends. Instead, it puts all its profits back into the company so that it can grow even bigger.*

Not exactly. Owning a share of stock in a company means that you own a part of that company—a piece of the action, so to speak. As one of the owners, you're entitled to a share of the money your company makes after all its expenses are paid—its profits. If you're a shareholder in Nike, for example, you stand to profit each time someone buys a pair of Nike sneakers. If you're a stockholder in Toys 'R' Us, you stand to profit every time someone buys a toy at one of its stores.

Profits are paid out in the form of a dividend, which is like the interest you earn on a bank account. Banks promise to pay you a certain rate of interest. Dividends, on the other hand, aren't guaranteed. The size of a dividend all depends on how much money the company makes. Sometimes even a profitable company doesn't pay dividends. Instead, it puts all its profits back into the company so that it can grow even bigger (Microsoft is a good example of a company like this).

When you're a stockholder, you can make money in another way, too. If your company does well and its stock becomes more valuable, the price of your shares will go up. If you paid $15 for a share of stock, for example, it might go up to $20 or even higher.

On the other hand, your company may not make much money, or could even *lose* money. If that's the case, it may not pay a dividend, and the price of a share of stock could fall from, say, $15 to $10 or less. That's the risk of investing in the stock market.

# "Can kids buy stocks?"

## Dr. T:

Yes, they can. Minor children (usually children under the age of 18) can't own stock directly. But all you have to do is ask your parents to fill out a simple form to open a custodial account—which means their name appears on the account along with yours.

With their parents' help, children can buy shares in any of the thousands of companies whose stock is bought and sold on stock exchanges, such as the New York Stock Exchange (NYSE), the NASDAQ market or the American Stock Exchange (AMEX). Once you have opened an account with a stockbroker (a person who buys and sells stocks for customers), all you have to do is call your broker and tell him or her how many shares of which company you'd like to buy.

# "How much does stock cost?"

## Dr. T:

The price is set by the market, and it all depends on how much buyers and sellers think the stock is worth that day. Some stocks sell for less than $10 a share, others for more than $100 a share. If you're interested in buying stock in a particular company, you can check to see how much its stock has been selling for by looking up the company alphabetically in the stock tables section of any newspaper. Stock tables have lots of small type and look long and boring, but they're really pretty easy to use once you know what you're looking for. (For some instructions on reading the stock tables, see page 125.)

*With their parents' help, children can buy shares in any of the thousands of companies whose stock is bought and sold on stock exchanges.*

# "Will I have to pay the stockbroker to buy shares of stock for me?"

## Dr. T:

Yes, you will. You'll be charged a fee, called a commission. Sometimes the commission is a percentage of the price you pay for the stock. Sometimes it's a flat fee. For kids, who will probably be buying or selling small amounts of stock, commissions can be expensive. Some stockbrokers may not even accept orders below a certain number of shares. You'll probably need your parents' help to find a broker willing to handle your account for a reasonable price.

Parents, take note: There *are* ways to help your kids keep commissions to a minimum. If you already have a brokerage account of your own, your broker may be willing to give your kids a break on commissions as a courtesy to you. Or you can open an account for your child with a discount broker.

Discount brokers won't give you advice on which stock to buy, but they will charge you less than so-called full-service brokers. For example, the firm of Kennedy, Cabot and Co. (800–252–0090) charges a flat fee of $23 to buy anywhere from one to 99 shares of stock. Through National Discount Brokers (http://pawws.com/ndb), you can buy shares online for a flat fee of $20 for a NASDAQ trade, or you can buy up to 5,000 shares for $25 (plus $3 postage) for a trade on the New York or American exchange. To open an account for kids, all you have to do is check the "Custodian for Minor" box on the standard new-account form.

About two dozen companies, including Exxon, Mobil and Dial (the soap company), will sell you shares of stock directly, bypassing brokers altogether. For a complete list of these companies, see the *Directory of Companies Offering Dividend Reinvestment Plans*, edited by Sumie Kinoshita and available for $29.95

(plus $2.50 shipping) from Evergreen Enterprises, P.O. Box 763, Laurel, MD 20725–0763.

You can also avoid commissions by investing through the Low Cost Investment Plan of the National Association of Investors Corp., P.O. Box 220, Royal Oak, MI 48068; 810–583–6242. With this plan, you can buy one or more shares of stock in more than 160 participating companies for the share price plus $7 per company. NAIC membership costs $39 a year.

## How to Read the Stock Listings

**A** A small "s" next to the listing means the stock was split or the company issued a stock dividend within the last year. This is your signal that the year's high and low prices have been adjusted to reflect the effect of the split.

**B** An "x" indicates that the stock has gone "ex-dividend." Investors who buy the stock now won't get the next dividend payment, which has been declared but not paid. Most listings stick the "x" next to the figure in the volume column.

**C** Sometimes a stock has been issued so recently that it doesn't have a full year's history on which to base its pricing. In such a case the 52-week high and low prices date from the beginning of trading and the stock gets a little "n" to the left of the listing.

**D** The dividend listed is the latest annual dividend paid by that stock.

**E** The yield is the stock's latest annual dividend expressed as a percentage of that day's price.

**F** The price/earnings ratio is the price of the stock divided by the earnings reported by the company for the latest four quarters.

**G** Prices—and price changes—are reported in ⅛-point increments. An eighth of a dollar is 0.125 cent.

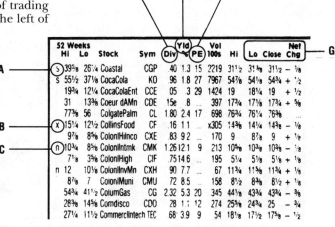

*Listing taken from the Wall Street Journal*

125

# "What happens after I buy a share of stock?"

## Dr. T:

You can follow its price in the stock tables in your newspaper, and listen or read news reports about how well the company is doing. The company will send you an annual report of its earnings and other important information.

Some companies give their shareholders extra perks. Wrigley sends stockholders a box of gum once a year. Tandy gives a 10% discount on Radio Shack computers, toys and games. Disney lets its shareholders buy a Magic Kingdom Club Gold Card, which entitles them to a slew of discounts at Disney resorts and theme parks.

You'll probably also be paid a dividend (which, remember, is a share of the company's profits). The dividend is decided on by the company's officers and is usually paid four times a year. In one family of investors, the kids are allowed to keep their dividends and use them as spending money. But you can also reinvest your dividends automatically in additional shares of the company's stock. That's a good idea for kids because it lets you buy more shares without paying a commission or even coming up with more cash of your own. Hundreds of companies offer dividend reinvestment plans, also known as DRIPs. For a complete listing, see the *Directory of Companies Offering Dividend Reinvestment Plans* noted on page 124.

*Calvin and Hobbes © 1995 Watterson. Dist. by Universal Press Syndicate. Reprinted with permission. All rights reserved.*

# "How do I choose which stock I want to buy?"

### Dr. T:

The first rule of good stock-picking is to invest in what you know. Start by making a list of companies whose products you buy or use—Coca-Cola, PepsiCo, McDonald's, Wendy's, Hershey, Toys "R" Us, Disney, Microsoft, The Learning Company, Nike, The Gap, just to name a few possibilities.

Once you have a list of likely candidates, you can narrow it down by looking up reports on the companies in sources that are available to the public either through your library or via online services. For example, your library will almost certainly have a copy of the *Value Line Investment Survey*, which provides full-page reports on about 1,700 stocks. You can also get access to Value Line on CompuServe through its Publications Online area.

As we discussed earlier, the price per share of any stock is determined by the market, and some stocks are more expensive than others. A stock that's selling for, say, $90 a share may be too rich for a kid's pocketbook. But it may be just the thing for grandparents who want to get their grandchildren interested in investing, start them off with a college savings fund or buy them a gift they won't outgrow or get bored with.

Dr. T doesn't recommend that you invest in "penny stocks," which typically sell for less than $1 a share. Sure, your limited budget will buy a lot of shares. But penny stocks are issued by companies that don't have much of a track record and aren't listed on any stock exchange. Investing is risky enough without stacking the deck against yourself.

# "How do I sell a stock?"

### Dr. T:

The same way you buy one, only backwards. You call your broker and tell him or her to sell your shares. You'll get the market price of the stock that day.

But you shouldn't get into the habit of selling stocks frequently. You'll have to pay a commission on each sale, just as you do when you buy a stock. And that could eat up any profits you might have made if the stock has gone up in price.

## How Many Francs to the Dollar?

Americans use dollars, but people in other countries use different kinds of money, such as rubles in Russia or francs in France. Who decides how many rubles or francs a dollar is worth?

The value of a dollar can change every day, and it's decided in an open market by people who actually buy and sell money. In this way, the currency market is much like the stock market or even a flea market.

To understand how this works, it helps to think of money itself as the product that's being bought and sold. Suppose you're planning a trip to Paris. You'll have to pay for your hotel, your fancy French pastries, and your tickets on the Metro (the Paris subway), but in France they don't take dollars, they take francs. So before you leave home you'll have to buy francs for the trip from a bank or a money exchange.

The bank gets its francs from traders all over the world who are linked by computer.

How many francs will a dollar buy? It all depends on how many francs the traders are willing to sell. If they are eager to get dollars—maybe because they want to buy American products, or because they just like the idea of owning dollars—they may be willing to make you an attractive offer of, say, six francs for a dollar. In that case, we say that the dollar is "strong."

But if they aren't very interested in buying dollars—maybe because they already have enough and don't want any more — they may offer you only four francs for your dollar. In that case, we say that the dollar is "weak"—and your trip just got more expensive, because you have to spend more dollars to get the francs you need.

# "But what if the price of my stock goes down?"

## Dr. T:

That can be an even better reason not to sell. The price of your stock is almost guaranteed to fall at some time. Maybe your company will go through a period when business isn't so great. Sometimes the whole stock market goes down because people are less enthusiastic about holding stocks.

But the best way to make money in the stock market is to buy shares in good companies that have the potential to grow, and hold on to them. Over time the stock market tends to rise, with downward blips along the way. When a stock price drops, young investors should follow the same strategy as adults: Ask yourself if you still like the company and think its future looks good. If the answer is no, go ahead and sell your shares. If the answer is yes, hold on—and maybe even buy some more.

"There goes Rodney. He made some shrewd investments with his milk money when he was in kindergarten."

*Hoest / Cartoonists & Writers Syndicate*

Remember the secret to making money in the stock market: Buy low, sell high. It may take a while for prices to rise again. But if anyone qualifies as a long-term investor who can ride out ups and downs in the market, it's a 12-year-old.

# "Who is Dow Jones? They talk about him on TV a lot."

### Dr. T:

Actually, your question should be "Who *are* Dow Jones?" "Dow" is Charles H. Dow and "Jones" is Edward D. Jones. In the 1880s they founded the newspaper that later became *The Wall Street Journal*.

In 1896 Mr. Dow began calculating the average daily price of 12 stocks. By the 1920s, the editors of *The Wall Street Journal* were tracking the stock prices of 30 big industrial companies every day. The 30 stocks chosen are representative of the broad market and of American industry.

What the editors did was add up the 30 stock prices and divide by a number to get an average price (it gets complicated here because they didn't divide by 30, but you don't have to worry about that). The average price they came up with was called the Dow Jones Industrial Average (or Dow, for short). Looking at movements in the average was a way of measuring whether the stock market as a whole went up or down. A rising Dow means stock prices went up; a falling Dow means they went down.

The Dow Jones Industrial Average became so popular that even after all these years, it's reported every day in the news. It's done by computer now, but the procedures are the same as those Charles Dow developed over a century ago, and a number of companies, including Sears and General Motors, have remained in the average since the 1920s.

By Bil Keane

"Daddy said he put a lot of money into our car. Let's go look for it."

4-12

*Reprinted with special permission of King Features Syndicate*

# "Wow! I just got a 3-D Cal Ripken Jr. baseball card! Is it going to be worth a lot of money some day?"

### You're tempted to say:
"If my mother had saved *my* baseball cards, we'd be millionaires today!"

### Dr. T's Rx:
Don't get your kids' hopes up too high when it comes to making money on baseball cards or any other collectible. Old baseball cards are valuable if there's interest in the players and if the cards are relatively rare and in mint condition. (That probably lets out most of your cards if you flipped them, stuffed them in your pockets or wrapped rubber bands around them. So don't blame your mother.)

Nowadays, with millions of cards being produced (and carefully preserved by kids with an eye to making a killing in the market), it's less likely that prices will shoot up in the future. Even if some do, it's tough to predict which players will generate the most interest a generation from now.

Tell your children to collect for love, not money. There's a market for just about anything you can collect—Barbie dolls, Hot Wheels cars, McDonald's Happy Meal toys—but markets are fickle. There's no guarantee you'll be able to sell your treasures at the time you want

| | Tennis Racquet (Performance line, frame only) | Basketball |
|---|---|---|
| **Prices Then & Now** | | |
| 1965 | $ 16.00 | $16.50 |
| 1975 | $ 29.00 | $29.00 |
| 1985 | $152.00 | $37.00 |
| Present | $185.00 | $52.00 |

Prices courtesy of Wilson Sporting Goods.
The materials used for tennis racquets have changed radically over the years. In 1965, virtually all racquets were wooden; by the mid 80s, racquets were mostly graphite composite.

To adjust earlier prices to account for the effects of inflation, multiply the 1965 prices by 5, the 1975 prices by 3 and the 1985 prices by 1.5.

*The real pleasure should come from the thrill of the chase that comes with building and enjoying a collection.*

the money and for the price you think they're worth. Kids, especially, can be taken advantage of. There are success stories, of course—like the young man who got hooked on collecting comic books when he was 4 and at 18 sold his collection of 10,000 books for $6,000, enough to pay for his first three semesters of college.

But any money you eventually make should be an unexpected bonus; the real pleasure should come from the thrill of the chase that comes with building and enjoying a collection.

So Mom and Dad, if your kids still harbor the hope that some day all that work will pay off, the best you can do is encourage them to:

- **Focus on items popular with kids between the ages of 10 and 17.** That's the time in their lives they'll try to recapture when they're 30; they won't remember much before the age of 8.

- **Treat collections gently.** Better still, if you have the space and the cash, buy duplicates of some items— one to play with and one to keep in its box. The container can easily double an item's value.

- **Look for collectibles with tie-ins to movie or television characters or well-known personalities,** whether it's Ronald McDonald or G.I. Joe. That's what makes an item memorable.

# The Teen Scene

The older they get, the higher the stakes. As toddlers at the grocery store your kids clamored for cookies. As teenagers they're agitating for cars and credit cards.

Suddenly faced with big-time demands on their budgets, parents are often in shock. They stall for time or just give up—anything to avoid saying no to argumentative teens who aren't inclined to give up without a fight. Sometimes it's tempting to take the easy way out and tell kids to get a job and pay for it all themselves.

But whether you and your children like it or not, you're still in charge. The best way to head off confrontations is to set a pattern of discussing money issues with your children when they're young so that you're still communicating when they're teens—and they're not surprised to hear you set standards about how their money will be spent, or just say no. But if you're already there, here's advice on how to handle your teenager's most common requests.

# "You're going to buy me a car when I'm 16, aren't you?"

### *You're tempted to say:*

"I can't believe you're almost old enough to drive."

### *Dr. T's Rx:*

Not so very long ago teens assumed their parents owed them a learner's permit on their 16th birthday. Nowadays teens assume their parents owe them a car. You don't.

If they get one at all, they should at least be required to help pay for it in some way. It's better to match whatever the kids save toward the purchase price than to buy the car yourself or even lend your kids the money (which has a way of not being paid back). If your kids don't have access to that kind of money, you might work out an arrangement in which you provide the wheels in exchange for your teens taking on the responsibility of running errands or chauffeuring younger siblings.

What children—and parents—often don't realize, however, is that buying the car is just the begin-

*FOXTROT copyright 1995 Bill Amend. Reprinted with permission of Universal Press Syndicate. All rights reserved.*

ning. Owning wheels is a long-term commitment that includes insurance, gasoline, routine maintenance and major repairs. The question "Will you buy me a car?" leads to "I need a new brake job" (see the following question). You need to work out ahead of time who's going to pay for what. Basic maintenance and gasoline should be your children's responsibility. Bigger expenses, especially emergency ones involving safety, might be shared.

One thirtysomething man recalls that when he owned a car as a teenager, the first thing he learned to do was change the oil himself. If he needed or wanted parts that were beyond his budget, he'd ask for them as gifts—sort of like "All I want for Christmas is two new front tires."

No matter how you divvy up the costs, teens will almost certainly need to get a part-time job to cover the expense of owning and maintaining a car—and working may not always be in their best interest (see Chapter 12).

Money isn't the only issue here; maturity is important, too. One family counselor says that in his experience it's better for adolescents to have use of an extra family car than to have one of their own. "I have found that the nicest of adolescents become rigid, selfish, demanding and difficult when they discuss 'their' car versus the 'family' car," he says. Also, it's less awkward for kids to explain to their friends that they've been grounded or can't get use of the car if it's a case of family ownership.

---

## Prices Then & Now

| | | |
|---|---|---|
| 1960s | Deluxe 3-speed Stingray bicycle | $ 82.95 |
| 1970s | BMX Scrambler bicycle | $116.95 |
| Present | 6-speed Thrasher bicycle | $229.00 |

*To adjust earlier prices to account for the effects of inflation, multiply the 1960s price by 5 and the 1970s price by 3.*

*Prices courtesy of Schwinn, Inc.*

---

**If it takes your kids a while to scrape together the cash they need to take the wheel, so much the better.**

# "Car insurance is so expensive! Will you pay for it?"

### You're tempted to say:
"Welcome to the real world."

### Dr. T's Rx:
Now that your teens are in the real world, they'll learn how to work out the best deal they can with both you and the insurance company.

You might agree to pay for insurance if your kids agree to drive one of the family cars instead of owning their own. Adding a teenager to your policy can easily double your premium, but the cost will be even higher if your teen owns her own car. Or maybe you'll contribute to the cost of the car but turn insurance and all other ongoing expenses over to your kids. One father paid his son's insurance for six months—long enough for the boy to get a job and make the payments himself. The point is, neither the car nor the related expenses should be a giveaway.

If it takes your kids a while to scrape together the cash they need to take the wheel, so much the better. Teens age 16 are injured in crashes 14.7 times per million miles traveled by that age group. That figure drops to 10.2 for 17-year-olds. One dad paid his daughter $50 for every month she put off getting her license, figuring the extra peace of mind was worth it.

One way to save money on insurance is to choose an older vehicle with low resale value, so you can skip comprehensive and collision coverage. You shouldn't cut corners on liability coverage, but you may qualify for discounts if your child is an occasional driver (driving the cars on your policy less than half the time); is a good student (in the top fifth of the class, on the honor roll or has at least a B average); has completed a driver's education course; or is a nonresident student away at a college or boarding school at least 100 miles from home without a car.

# "The French Club is going to Quebec for spring break. Can I go (and will you pay for it)?"

or

# "The French Club is going on a ski trip for spring break. Can I go (and will you pay for it)?"

### You're tempted to say:

"Don't you kids spend any time in school?"

### Dr. T's Rx:

Your observation may be on target, but you're giving equal weight to two very different requests—and giving your kids hope that you will, in fact, come up with the scratch.

If the trip in question is part of the academic curriculum, as in the first example, you should probably be more inclined to let your kids go. But you shouldn't feel obliged to pay the full freight. Any kind of class trip should include class fundraising. Beyond that, your children will appreciate the experience more if they have to come up with some cash of their own, even if it's just in the form of spending money.

If the trip in question is purely social, as in the second case, there are less compelling reasons to let your child go—and no reason at all to pay for it. Teenagers should expect to finance a trip like this from their allowance, savings and money they earn from a part-time job.

*Making kids responsible for the bulk of the prom bill puts an automatic limit on expenses that have a tendency to get out of hand.*

# 66The prom is going to be really expensive. You're going to help me pay for it, aren't you?99

### You're tempted to say:
"I am?"

### Dr. T's Rx:

Remember Dr. T's rules of dating etiquette: Whoever does the asking should expect to pick up the tab, and whoever picks up the tab should do it with his or her own money.

Dr. T can also be flexible on occasion, and the prom is one of those occasions. It's such a big event in a teenager's life, and such a big expense, that you can justify helping out. For instance, parents could certainly pay for the prom dress or tux, which, after all, counts as clothing (although kids who get a clothing allowance sometimes go it alone. One teen bought a dress two sizes too big on sale at Bloomingdale's for $35, and Mom paid for alterations).

But making kids responsible for the bulk of the bill puts an automatic limit on expenses that have a tendency to get out of hand. It can also inspire some creative alternatives. The pre-prom dinner moves from a splashy restaurant with attitude to a quieter one with atmosphere. The rented limo becomes expendable. One PTA sponsored a successful used-dress sale. "When my friends were shopping for a dress, they always had in mind whether they'd be able to wear it again," says one practical teen, who has worn her own prom dress several times.

Dr. T also hears via the teen grapevine that it's cool for a couple to split the cost of a major event like this one. One senior who invited a boy to her prom paid for the tickets, while he picked up the tab for dinner.

In Dr. T's opinion, neither parents nor children should be laying out money for a hotel room, and that's a matter of principle as much as price. To discourage the practice, one high school moved its prom venue from the hotel scene altogether, and class officers chose a local dance club instead. Tickets were a reasonable $15 per person because the class covered much of the cost through fundraisers.

Perhaps the best way to keep expenses under control is for parents to take an active role in prom planning. They can host at-home pre-prom dinners or after-prom parties and breakfasts (supervised, of course) and have no trouble attracting kids. "I had 50 willing guests in my house after the prom," says one parent. "In my circle of friends parents were always a part of things, so it was expected," says her daughter. At many schools parents sponsor all-night parties, with movies in the auditorium, karaoke in the gym, and a breakfast buffet in the cafeteria. For as little as $10 per ticket, it's the best deal in town.

*By permission of Mell Lazarus and Creators Syndicate*

*Just as children need to walk before they run, they need to learn how to manage cash before they can manage credit.*

# "Can I use your credit card?"

### You're tempted to say:
"Over my dead body."

### Dr. T's Rx:
You're on the right track, although Dr. T hopes that such drastic measures won't be necessary.

There is an argument to be made for letting teens under 18 use your card. That way you can get a look at the bills as they come in, and make sure your kids pay their share. Many parents swear by such a system.

But Dr. T isn't one of them. Just as children need to walk before they run, they need to learn to manage cash before they can manage credit. Giving your kids a seasonal clothing allowance several times a year will do more to develop their money management skills than giving them a credit card. Once they've mastered the discipline of living within a cash budget, you won't have to worry so much about them losing their heads when they get a credit card of their own.

# "Can I have my own credit card?"

### You're tempted to say:
"Over my dead body."

### Dr. T's Rx:
This tactic won't work indefinitely. Once your kids turn 18, and especially if they go off to college, they'll probably be able to get a pocketful of credit cards without your permission, or even your knowledge. Your best hope is that they're smart enough about handling money that they don't pull any of the top three stupid college tricks:

- **Treating the gang.** Out for an evening of pizza, they pick up the tab on their card, collect each kid's share in cash—and then spend the cash.

- **Digging a hole.** They rack up a big balance and then make only the minimum payment—a surefire way never to get out of debt.

- **Letting things slide.** They're afraid to confess that they can't make the payments on time, and that makes things worse. Late payments can stay on their credit report for years, hurting their ability to get additional loans or land a job.

However, you might want your college kids to have a credit card, if only for emergencies. To head off problems, you might steer your kids toward a secured credit card, which will require them to deposit money in a savings account with the bank that issues the card. The credit line is equal to the amount of the deposit, which should keep the kids from getting in over their heads and teach them that credit has a cost.

Another alternative is for you to be the primary borrower on the card, with your child as co-signer or co-borrower. That way you'd see the bills, but your child would get the opportunity to build an independent credit history. (A word of caution: If your name is going to appear on your child's account, it's better for you to be the primary borrower than the co-signer. Card issuers and other creditors have no obligation to notify co-signers when the primary borrower isn't making payments. So your child's spotty payment history could turn up on your credit record as well, without your knowledge.)

For a lecture on credit that doesn't come from Mom and Dad, there's *Smart Credit Strategies for College Students,* an audiotape from Good Advice Press ($15.95; 800–255–0899).

# "What do you mean you can't afford to send me to a college that costs $20,000 a year? Haven't you been saving the money?"

**You're tempted to say:**
"Aaaargh!"

**Dr. T's Rx:**
You may *have* been saving money, but if you have other priorities you're not obliged to spend it all on college tuition. Even if you're willing to do that, your children should never take it for granted. Get them involved in college planning as soon as they become teenagers so they have an idea of how much you can afford and how much you expect them to contribute. Neither of you should be surprised later.

# Losses & Loans & Penalties, Oh My!

**E**very day your children will pose puzzling questions that don't conveniently fit into any category–except perhaps the normal give and take of family life. Should you give your kids money as a reward for good grades, or take it away as punishment if they misbehave? If your children lose the money you gave them to buy something, should you give them more? Should you let your kids borrow money from each other? What if they forget to pay it back?

It isn't always easy to come up with a solution that satisfies everyone, and parents are bound to disagree. Take the issue of payment for grades. One survey showed that 40% of Americans felt that kids should be rewarded for academic achievement, and 58% said they shouldn't. But of those surveyed, parents were more likely than non-parents to say kids should receive cash for good grades.

In this chapter Dr. T offers guidance on how to smooth over family disputes–and how to calculate just how much the tooth fairy should bring.

# "How much will the tooth fairy bring me?"

### *You're tempted to say:*
"In my day the going rate was 10 cents a tooth."

### *Dr. T's Rx:*

The tooth fairy is an easygoing sprite who's willing to tailor her gifts to your wishes, so almost any pricing strategy will do. Dr. T offers a few guidelines:

- **Forget 10 cents a tooth.** A dime just doesn't go very far these days, even for a 5-year-old. The tooth fairy would be happy to give anywhere from 25 cents to $1. Remember, losing a mouthful of teeth is a long-term proposition. You could start with a quarter for those first itty-bitty bottom teeth and build up to $1 for the molars your kids will still be losing at age 11 or 12.

| Prices Then & Now | | |
|---|---|---|
| 1960 | Monopoly set | $ 4 |
| 1970 | Monopoly set | $ 8 |
| Present | Monopoly set | $12 |

*To adjust earlier prices to account for the effects of inflation, multiply the 1960 price by 5 and the 1970 price by 4.*

*Prices courtesy of Parker Brothers, Inc.*

- **Take advantage of the tooth fairy's flexibility.** Instead of an ordinary coin, have her bring something special, such as a Kennedy half-dollar or a silver dollar. Then the tooth coins will stand out from the other money in the piggy bank, and your kids will be less inclined to spend them.

- **The tooth fairy will be happy to bring stickers, erasers or other small tokens,** if you think the whole tooth-for-money exchange is too mercenary.

# **"How come you always take my money to pay the pizza man or the baby sitter?"**

### *You're tempted to say:*

"We don't *always* take your money."

### *Dr. T's Rx:*

Well, maybe not always. But tell your children the truth: Parents often borrow spare change from their kids because their kids are the only ones who ever seem to have any. It goes with being part of a family. If parents can learn to put up with little annoyances like kids who leave wet towels on the bathroom floor, kids can learn to put up with parents who raid their cash stash.

However, kids do have a right to be paid back in a timely fashion. Parents don't intentionally neglect to repay the money; it just slips their mind. Consider this a friendly reminder and an opportunity to clear your conscience. Before you go on to the next question, give your daughter the $5 you owe her.

## *Small Change*

• • • • • • • • • • • • • • • • • • • • • • • •

Foreign coins were officially a legal part of the American monetary system from 1793 until 1857. However, Spanish coins remained in wide use in the Southwest, and many Americans hoarded them and used them during the Civil War coin shortage.

*Brother or sister
also needs to be
taught the
consequences
of failing to
repay a debt.*

## "[Insert name of brother or sister] always borrows money from me and never pays me back. What should I do?"

### You're tempted to say:
"That'll teach you not to lend him/her money any more."

### Dr. T's Rx:
That's only part of the lesson to be learned. Brother or sister also needs to be taught the consequences of failing to repay a debt.

Take both siblings aside and explain the meaning of the word "deadbeat." Then lay down the house rules about borrowing, which might go something like this: Henceforth, any loan of petty cash is expected to be repaid within, say, one week of the date borrowed. After that, interest will start to accrue at the rate of a nickel a day. If the loan is still outstanding after two weeks, you'll deduct the money from the borrower's allowance and tell his or her sibling not to advance any more cash.

It may sound a little drastic, but the idea is to get the delinquent sibling to shape up. And you may never have to charge any interest or cut off a kid's credit. When one parent outlined the house rules to his children, the $3 big brother had borrowed weeks before mysteriously turned up on little sister's dresser within hours.

Dr. T doesn't object in principle to siblings lending money to one another as long as neither the borrower nor the lender is being exploited.

## "I lost the $20 you gave me to rent a videotape. Can I have more money?"

*If a child loses money by accident rather than by habit, there's no need to rub salt into the wounds.*

### You're tempted to say:

"This time *I'll* pay for the tape."

### Dr. T's Rx:

Unless you want to see the tape yourself, head home without it. The lost money was your child's responsibility, and you're under no obligation to make up the loss.

Having said that, Dr. T is willing make an exception if your child is sufficiently chastened. Dr. T once heard from a young woman who vividly recalled an incident from her youth, in which she lost the money her mother had given her to go to the grocery store. "I felt awful, and just having to go home and confess was worse than any punishment my mother could have inflicted." If your child has scoured the video store for the missing money and is obviously upset about the loss, go ahead and rent the tape. If a child loses money by accident rather than by habit, there's no need to rub salt into the wounds.

That's especially true if you're partly at fault. Parents shouldn't get into the habit of peeling off $20 bills to give their children. Young children especially feel uncomfortable about carrying that much cash. Not only do they worry about losing it, but they also worry about losing the change—or being cheated by a dishonest sales clerk because they're little kids. Give your child an amount of money that more closely matches the purchase price. If you don't have anything smaller than a $20 bill, pay for the tape (or whatever) yourself.

# "I lost my library book and they're charging me $10. Will you pay it?"

**You're tempted to say:**
"I'm not the one who lost the book."

**Dr. T's Rx:**

In a situation as clear-cut as this one, not even your children should seriously expect you to come up with the cash. But make sure your kids understand that the fine won't go unpaid. If they don't have the money right away, they'll have to save it out of their allowance or do extra chores to earn it.

When kids lose money they feel the impact immediately. When they lose something other than money, the financial consequences aren't always as direct. It can take time, and a little effort on your part, to get the point across. A couple of other situations:

- **Your son tries out for football but quits,** carelessly leaving his uniform in his locker instead of turning it in. A month later you get a $150 bill for a lost uniform. Your son doesn't have $150, and it would take too long to work off a debt that size. The school wants its money now. Advance your son the cash, but deduct $5 a week from his allowance until the loan is repaid (or let him do extra chores to work off the debt more quickly).

- **For Christmas you bought your daughter the snazzy watch she'd had her eye on for months.** By Easter the watch is history, and your daughter is pining for a replacement. Let her pine. If you're willing to consider buying a new watch (and there's no reason why you should), at least make her wait until next Christmas. Absence may make the watch grow less attractive, or your daughter more careful.

## "Why do you always make us turn off the lights when we leave the room?"

*You're tempted to say:*

"Because we don't own the electric company."

### Dr. T's Rx:

Kids, even teens, are often in the dark about household expenses, and this old standby doesn't enlighten them much. Take a few more seconds to amplify your explanation.

Tell them you have to pay the power company for the electricity you use each month, just as you pay the gas company for heat, the telephone company, the cable TV company, the supermarket . . . and so on down the line. Since there's only so much money to go around, you don't want to pay anyone more than you have to. That way you'll have more money left for other things the kids might enjoy—like going out for pizza on Saturday night. Now you're speaking their language!

| Prices Then & Now | Converse All Stars | Nike |
|---|---|---|
| 1960s | $10.00 | |
| 1970s | $15.95 | $25.00 |
| 1980s | $26.50 | $55.00 |
| Present | $33.00 | $100.00 |

*To adjust earlier prices to account for the effects of inflation, multiply the 1960s prices by 5, the 1970s prices by 3 and the 1980s prices by 1.5.*

*Buying grades, or any other good behavior, distracts kids from the sense of accomplishment that should be their real reward.*

## "How much will you pay me if I get good grades on my report card?"

### You're tempted to say:
"How about $2 per 'A'?"

### Dr. T's Rx:

In their heart of hearts, parents suspect that they shouldn't be rewarding their kids' academic efforts with money. But they want their children to do well in school, and if coming across with some cash will do the trick, they figure it's a small price to pay.

Bag the cash. Pay the kids a compliment, pay the tuition at the college their good grades will get them into, but don't pay them money. Buying grades, or any other good behavior, distracts kids from the sense of accomplishment that should be their real reward. Besides, it can get expensive. And if you're trying to control your children's behavior with money you're doomed to failure, because eventually they can go out and earn their own.

Dr. T does know of cases in which parents have successfully used money as compensation for grades. One dad worked out a complex set of financial incentives that rewarded his 11-year-old son for improved grades, even if they weren't As. A mom set aside time every week to go over school papers with her first-grader and paid him $1 for every 100%. But money seems to work best as a motivator when it's used in small amounts over limited periods of time; the longer you do it, the less effective it is. Your goal should be to wean kids from cash just as you eventually weaned them from treats when they learned to go to the potty.

Even in the situations noted above, factors other than money were at work. In the first case, the 11-year-old admitted that he was also influenced by a conscientious teacher who prodded him to get better grades. In the second case, Mom's interest and approval probably had as much of an effect on her son's performance as the money. Paying a compliment will buy better results than paying cash.

While promising a reward ahead of time is risky, a spontaneous blowout after the fact to celebrate a good report card is always a morale booster. Go ahead, treat your scholar to a banana split, or even dinner at the restaurant of his or her choice.

## "How much will you pay me to stay out of the way during your party tonight?"

### Dr. T's Rx:

Dr. T fervently hopes that you're not going to dignify this one with *any* answer. Rewarding your children for doing something good is tricky enough; paying them off for not doing something bad is simply *blackmail*.

| Prices Then & Now | | |
|---|---|---|
| 1960s | Records | $5–$7 |
| 1970s | Records | $7 |
| 1980s | Cassette tapes | $8–$10 |
| Present | Compact discs | $12–$20 |

*To adjust earlier prices to account for the effects of inflation, multiply the 1960s price by 5, the 1970s price by 4 and the 1980s price by 1.5.*

*Docking an allowance is an old standby but other punishments usually fit the crime more closely and can be even easier to enforce.*

## "How come you're docking my allowance just because I wouldn't let Peter watch his TV show?"

### *You're tempted to say:*
"Because I'm sick and tired of hearing the two of you fight."

### *Dr. T's Rx:*

Dr. T is tempted to agree with the kids on this one. What does fighting over the television have to do with their allowance?

Docking an allowance is an old standby, but other punishments usually fit the crime more closely and can be even easier to enforce. If you're sick of listening to your kids fight over what to watch on television, don't let them watch anything until they can work out a schedule they both agree on.

Just as using money as a reward can work in certain limited, well-defined situations, using money as a penalty can work, too. Parents sometimes succeed in changing their kids' behavior by telling the kids that certain no-nos—forgetting to do an assigned chore, leaving dirty dishes in the family room—will result in a fine. But in cases like these the fines are usually announced in advance instead of being imposed on the spur of the moment because you couldn't think of anything better to do.

It is appropriate to dock your child's allowance if the "crime" costs money—your son breaks a window with a soccer ball or loses his orthodontic retainer, for instance. One 13-year-old girl ran up a long-distance phone bill of nearly $500 while on a class trip. When she got home, her father made her pay off the bill in part by deducting half of her allowance until the debt was paid (he also took half of her birthday money).

# "Can I give all my money away to poor people?"

### You're tempted to say:
[Embarrassed silence.]

### Dr. T's Rx:

Admirable though it may be, the impulse of some children to give away all their money is as unrealistic as wanting to spend it all on toys for themselves. And other children can take unfair advantage of their generosity. Caught without exact change, one mom and dad sent their 8-year-old to school with a $5 bill to pay for a $2 lunch. When the girl's friends asked her for money, she didn't have the heart to say no, and ended up giving away all the change.

The trick is to bring kids down to earth without dashing their spirit. In the case above, Mom and Dad sat down with their daughter and explained that they needed the change from the $5 to help buy groceries for dinner, or pay for the next day's lunch, or buy school supplies—expenses that an 8-year-old could understand. A week or so later, they deliberately sent their daughter off to school with a $5 bill in her wallet and a reminder to bring home the change. She did.

In order to grow up with a healthy attitude toward money, kids need to learn that it's a tool with lots of uses. Just as overspenders need to be prodded into saving money, overgivers need to have their charitable instincts channeled. Help them focus on a favorite cause that appeals to them, preferably one that's in your community so the kids can take their money there themselves or donate their outgrown toys and clothing.

*The trick is to bring kids down to earth without dashing their spirit.*

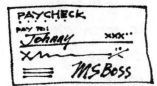
# The World of Work

**W**ith your kids spending so much of your money, you probably live for the day when they can start making some of their own. Tempted by the appealing prospect of extra income, it's easy for both parents and kids to lose perspective. When kids are older, parents can be too quick to push them out the door and behind the nearest fast-food counter when they should be at home hitting the books.

On the other hand, when children are younger and beg to set up a lemonade stand, parents sometimes discourage them for fear that it will be too much work for mom and dad. As a result, younger kids can end up working too little, and older kids too much. Here's how to strike a balance.

# "Why do athletes and movie stars get paid so much money?"

### You're tempted to say:
"Because they're greedy."

### Dr. T's Rx:
That may be so, but it doesn't do much to advance your child's knowledge of labor economics. It may be hard to accept the fact that sports stars earn more than teachers, but it isn't hard to explain.

It's just a simple matter of supply and demand for workers. There's a big demand on the part of team owners and fans for top players, but there's a very limited supply of Michaels, Shaqs and Hakeems. So their salaries are bid up. There's also a demand for teachers, of course, but many more people are available to fill those positions, so school districts aren't forced to bid up their salaries as high (nor could they afford to).

| Prices Then & Now | VCR | Camcorder |
|---|---|---|
| 1970s | $995–$1,100 | $1,500 |
| 1980s | $350–$900 | $1,200 |
| Present | $350–$450(stereo) | $500–$600 |

*To adjust earlier prices to account for the effects of inflation, multiply the 1970s price by 3 and the 1980s price by 1.5.*

Don't forget, though, that despite the glamor and the money, sports and movies are high-risk businesses. Team owners and movie producers expect superstars to more than pay for themselves by selling tickets. If a movie bombs, a star becomes a has-been. If a player is injured, his value plummets. Even if he stays healthy, he can be washed up by age 35.

In economic terms, players try to "maximize their income" before they're fully depreciated (used up) as an asset to their team. In other words, they try to make hay while the sun shines.

# "Why do you have to go to work every day?"

### *You're tempted to say:*

"To put bread on the table for you."

### *Dr. T's Rx:*

Your kids aren't likely to grasp your attempt at humor. They'll take you literally, and a response like this makes it sound as if you're literally a step away from starvation—and it's all their fault.

Tell your children instead that you work to earn money to pay for all the things your whole family needs and wants. Tell them you work to earn money to save for the future—to pay for next year's vacation, or a new car. Tell them you work because you're good at what you do. Tell them you work because you enjoy it.

Children don't always hear a dispassionate discussion of adult jobs. They're more likely to overhear you grousing about the boss or yearning for early retirement.

It's healthier for all of you to get your children involved with what you do. Take them to work on a regular work day so they know where you go every day. Talk about the people you work with and what your job involves.

You may spend more of your waking hours on the job than with your children. So anything you can do to make your kids feel more a part of your mysteri-

## Money Talks

• • • • • • • • • • • • • • • • • • • • • • • • •

A **"plugged (or plug) nickel,"** as in "not worth a plugged nickel," comes from the days when coins were made of precious metals like silver or gold. Sometimes people cheated by removing some of the silver and replacing it with a worthless plug. The nickel itself was never made out of a precious metal to begin with, so a "plugged nickel" was really worthless.

**"Wooden nickels,"** as in "Don't take any wooden nickels," referred literally to counterfeit coins made of wood, but came to have the friendly connotation, "Keep out of trouble." For a short time during the 1930s, wooden nickels actually had value, when they were issued by some towns in Washington state as a substitute for metal coins, which were in short supply. Once metal coins reappeared, however, the wooden ones weren't worth a plugged nickel.

ous outside life is bound to bring you closer together, make you less resentful of the time you spend apart, and make your children less fearful of the day when they'll have to go to work to put bread on the table.

You can also have a big influence on their career choices. One study of children from kindergarten to sixth grade showed that more of them wanted to follow in Mom's footsteps than in Dad's. Among fifth-graders, 33% of the girls—and 30% of the boys—said they wanted to have the same job as their mother. Only 11% of the girls, and 13% of the boys, cited their fathers' jobs. The study concluded that the kids choose Mom's field more often because women tell their children more about their jobs, and are more likely to take their children to the place they work.

One woman who runs a business out of her home even took her two children on a tour of her home office and carefully explained that that's where she goes to do her job and earn money. Several weeks later she mentioned that she was short on cash and would have to make a trip to the bank, when her son piped up, "Mommy, you can just go into your office and make some."

"That's fine son, but just remember that no one ever made a bundle tying knots."

© by Frank Tabor

## "What can I do to earn money this summer?"

*To keep up kids' enthusiasm, they need to be doing something that's manageable and fun.*

### You're tempted to say:

"I can look out my window and see a lawn that needs mowing."

### Dr. T's Rx:

For the 12-and-under crowd, earning money begins at home with jobs like mowing lawns or babysitting.

But don't stop there. Encourage your kids to think bigger and more creatively by asking the neighbors if they could use a hand with summer yard work, such as watering plants or hosing decks (anything that can be done outside with water is a hit with kids). That way they could build a bigger clientele and a steady income. Instead of waiting around for babysitting jobs on Saturday night, they could organize a daily dinnertime play group that gives harried parents an hour or two of free time.

Truth to tell, most kids would probably prefer to be bored than to work too hard over the summer. To keep up their enthusiasm, they need to be doing something that's manageable and fun.

Primary-school children still think in concrete terms—money can be exchanged for things. So they get a kick out of selling stuff, any stuff—old toys, pictures they draw, cookies they bake, and, yes, even lemonade.

You'll have to put in a little time helping them bake the cookies or choose sale items that they won't want back the next day. But you don't have to spend days constructing an elaborate stand or hours minding the store. The kids will be happy to sit by themselves at a card table in your front yard for an hour or two and make $5. Here's a twist: Let them sell lemonade at *your* yard sale.

Middle-school children between the ages of 9 and 13 are perfect for the service economy. They're old enough to take on jobs with a certain amount of responsibility and young enough to be enthusiastic about it. Summer lends itself to lots of possibilities: Feeding the cat and taking in the mail for neighbors who are on vacation; washing cars; lugging trash cans out to the curb each week.

One enterprising 12-year-old offered his services as waiter, busboy and gofer to an aunt who was giving a dinner party. Seven hours later he went home with $25 in his pocket. Two 10-year-olds set up shop doing hair braids for 25 cents each. They also offered a tie-dying service for birthday parties.

## Money Talks

● ● ● ● ● ● ● ● ● ● ● ● ● ● ● ● ● ● ● ● ● ●

Why do we call a dollar a "buck?"

The nickname may have come from the days before paper money, when Americans traded buckskins instead of cash. Let's trace the roots of some other money monikers:

- A "fin," or $5, probably comes from the Yiddish word finif or the German fünf, meaning five.

- A "sawbuck" is $10. At one point in U.S. history, the number ten on a $10 bill was represented by the Roman numeral X, which looked like a sawhorse.

- A "C-note" is a $100 bill, so-called for the Roman numeral C, meaning 100.

Your children will be happiest and most productive if they do something that taps their special talents or interests. If they're good at computers, they could tutor other kids, or adults, who need help. One brother-sister team shared a job reading aloud to a handicapped child in the neighborhood. If they're artistically inclined, they could make and sell jewelry or refrigerator magnets. One young lady made more than $100 during her summer at the beach by selling necklaces she made out of colorful fishing lures.

Young kids don't have wheels, but they don't need to go too far afield. They can make funky flyers and target likely customers in the neighborhood—families with young children who are in need of babysitters, or older people who'd appreciate having someone else haul their trash cans.

# "Can I get a part-time job after school?"

## You're tempted to say:

"It's about time you started earning some money of your own."

## Dr. T's Rx:

Don't be too quick to push teenagers into the workplace. At this age their first job is to be a student, and it would be a mistake to sacrifice future job prospects to a quick boost in discretionary income.

Studies have shown that teens who work less than ten hours a week actually get better grades, on average, than kids who don't work at all. But among teens who work more than 20 hours per week, grades begin to suffer, children have less contact with their parents (who also have less authority over the kids) and drug and alcohol use go up.

It's not clear from these studies whether long work hours caused grades to suffer, or whether kids who were already doing poorly in school decided to

### Prices Then & Now

| 1960s | 19" black & white television | $155 |
|---|---|---|
| 1970s | 19" color television | $475 |
| 1980s | 19" color television | $425–$600 |
| Present | 20" color television | $270–$350 |
| | Big-screen television | $600–$1,500 |

*To adjust earlier prices to account for the effects of inflation, multiply the 1960s price by 5, the 1970s price by 3 and the 1980s price by 1.5.*

put more time into paid work. It does seem that getting a jump on a job, especially in senior year, gives students who don't go on to college a leg up in the labor market. Years after graduation, they're still earning substantially more than classmates who didn't work as students and didn't go on to college.

But even in this case, small doses of work seem to yield big benefits. Whether or not your kids are college-bound, tell them they can get a part-time job if it's limited to around ten hours a week when they're sophomores, or 15 if they're juniors or seniors—with the proviso that they cut back the hours if grades suffer, or be allowed to work more if they seem able to handle it.

You're trying to strike a balance, as did the family in the following letter to Dr. T: "Several years ago our daughter volunteered at our local library during the summer. When she returned to high school, she was given the opportunity to work at the library 20 hours a week. We thought it would interfere with her studies, so we settled on 10 hours. She worked there for four years, through her second year of college.

"She developed a love for reading and became a history teacher for three years. Now she's an archivist at the National Archives in Washington."

If the idea of a job appeals to you as a way to help your children learn to assume responsibility and work with others, extracurricular activities and volunteer work can serve the same purpose. To encourage a son who wanted to be a doctor, one father offered to pay him what he would've earned flipping burgers if instead he volunteered at a hospital. He volunteered throughout high school, and eventually did enroll in medical school.

**FYI:** Child-labor laws limit the work hours of a 14- or 15-year-old to no more than 3 hours on a school day or 18 hours in a school week. But the law doesn't restrict working hours for children 16 and older.

*Kids are notorious for overpricing or underpricing their services, or not pricing them at all and letting their employers decide how much to pay them.*

# "The Thayers want me to babysit for them. How much should I charge?"

### You're tempted to say:
"I used to get paid 50 cents an hour."

### Dr. T's Rx:

Forget the nostalgia and contribute some market research. Until now *you've* probably been paying for babysitters, so you have some idea of the going rate, or some idea of what *you'd* be willing to pay for whatever service your children want to perform.

Kids are notorious for overpricing or underpricing their services, or not pricing them at all and letting their employers decide how much to pay them. Kids should always quote a price, even if it's negotiable. And they should check with other kids beforehand to see what the competition is charging. A certificate from a babysitting course could earn them a premium over the neighborhood rate. For some general guidance, here are the median earnings for a variety of summer jobs, as reported in a survey by *Zillions*, the consumer magazine for kids: Picking up mail for vacationing neighbors, $5 a week; babysitting, $3 an hour; lawn-mowing, $7 a lawn; car-washing, $4 a car ($3 more for a wax); watering yards, $3 a job. Yard sales netted $24 for the summer.

Should *you* pay your kids for doing some of these jobs? It depends. You shouldn't pay your 13-year-old to stay with younger siblings for an hour or so after school while you run errands. But you should expect to pay for a Saturday night job, since he or she could easily land a paying gig. You could, of course, negotiate for a family discount.

# "How come my paycheck is smaller than it should be?"

### You're tempted to say:

"That's your government at work."

### Dr. T's Rx:

Don't be surprised if your kids are surprised that kids have to pay taxes, too. Warn them that even though they're teenagers working part-time for $5 an hour, taxes will be withheld from their paychecks.

They'll probably be able to get most of the money back, however, by filing a tax return and waiting for a refund. Children claimed as dependents on their parents' tax return can claim up to the same standard deduction as a single person, or the total of their earned income, whichever is less.

**Note:** Social security taxes are not refundable.

*Reprinted with special permission of King Features Syndicate*

# CHAPTER 13

# Sensitive Issues, Sensible Solutions

**S**ome of the toughest questions kids ask are only partly about money. When they wonder why you and your spouse always fight over money, they're also asking about your relationship with your spouse or worrying about their own security. Money may not be the root of the problem, but it's often the hot button that makes long-simmering tensions explode into the open. Your children fret, or try to take advantage of the situation by playing off one parent against the other.

Children of divorce are particularly vulnerable. Their parents may no longer live together, but money and the kids are still the ties that bind them. "Children of divorce know more about their parents' finances than any other group of children I've worked with," says one family counselor.

Even if you never talk to your kids directly about money, they're bound to pick up an earful by listening in on your discussions with your spouse. Always be conscious of the message you're sending.

# "Dad, can I have $15 for a new CD? Mom says no, but all the other kids have it."

### You're tempted to say:

"Sure, why not. Your mom is always pinching pennies."

### Dr. T's Rx:

Your child is trying to extort money from you by using the old divide and conquer technique (which has apparently worked for your child in the past if you have heard this question more than once).

Stand by your spouse. Tell your child that if Mom (or Dad) says no, the answer is no. There are lots of other issues here—whether you can afford the $15, whether you should cave in to your child's peer pressure, whether your child should be buying the CD with his or her own money (all of which are covered elsewhere in this book). But in a situation like this, your most important consideration is to keep up a united front. If you do, chances are you won't hear this question again. If you crack, your action (and your kid) will come back to haunt you.

If you really disagree with your spouse, or if your child is exploiting a sore spot between the two of you, you and your spouse should talk it over afterward to agree on a response. But this is one discussion that doesn't have to take place in front of the children.

| Prices Then & Now | | |
|---|---|---|
| 1960s | Wooden baseball bat | $5 |
| 1970s | Wooden baseball bat | $6 |
| Present | Aluminum baseball bat | $30-$40 |

*To adjust earlier prices to account for the effects of inflation, multiply the 1960s price by 5, the 1970s price by 3.*

# "Why do you two always fight about money?"

### You're tempted to say:

"We *don't* always fight about money."

### Dr. T's Rx:

That may be true, but your kids are obviously getting a different impression.

Don't overreact or go on the defensive. Instead, ask your children to describe a time when you and your spouse fought about money. What they define as "fighting" might simply be a run-of-the-mill parental discussion about whether to get the car fixed or buy a new one. If that's the case, you can reassure your kids by bringing them in on the discussion, which is critical anyway if they're ever to learn how to make such decisions themselves. If they're old enough to eavesdrop, they're old enough to participate.

It's just possible, of course, that you really *were* arguing. Show me a couple who don't fight about money, goes the old one-liner, and I'll show you a couple on the way to the altar. If that's the case, consider your kids' question a warning and use it as an opportunity to resolve your differences. For example, even among couples who tend to think alike about money, it's common for one spouse to want to spend and the other to play the role of spoiler. Instead of shouting at each other about who's spending too much on what, try putting down your dispute on paper. Go

"I've called the family together to announce that, because of inflation, I'm going to have to let two of you go."

*Farris/Cartoonists & Writers Syndicate*

over your paychecks and bills together to see how the numbers add up (or don't add up). Write down your financial goals—a major vacation, your children's education, retirement—to see whether you're on track toward achieving them. Once you see where you stand in dollars and cents, one spouse may be convinced that you need to spend less, or the other might feel more comfortable about spending more. "People are willing to change their behavior as long as they don't feel like they're being blamed," says one family counselor.

If, after all, your kids were right on target and you *are* always fighting about money, you may have to seek outside help from a group such as Debtors Anonymous (P.O. Box 400, Grand Central Station, New York, NY 10163–0400; 212–642–8220), or from a marriage mediator (see the box on page 172). "Fighting in front of the kids isn't bad as long as the kids see you finding a solution," says one mediator.

*Go over your paychecks and bills together to see how the numbers add up.*

## Money Around the World

| Currency | Country | Currency | Country | Currency | Country |
|---|---|---|---|---|---|
| Bolivar | Venezuela | Franc | Belgium, France, Switzerland (and others) | Pound | Egypt, Great Britain, Lebanon (and others) |
| Dinar | Algeria, Jordan, Kuwait (and others) | Forint | Hungary | | |
| Dirham | Morocco, United Arab Emirates | Guilder | Netherlands | Punt | Ireland |
| | | Koruna | Czech Republic, Slovak Republic | Rand | South Africa |
| | | | | Royal | Saudi Arabia |
| Dollar | Australia, Canada, Hong Kong, New Zealand, Singapore, United States (and others) | Krona | Iceland, Sweden | Ruble | Russia |
| | | Krone | Denmark, Norway | Rupee | India, Pakistan (and others) |
| | | Lira | Italy, Turkey | Schilling | Austria |
| | | Mark | Germany | Shekel *(new)* | Israel |
| | | Peseta | Spain | Sol | Peru |
| | | Peso | Argentina, Chile, Colombia, Mexico, Phillippines, Uruguay (and others) | Yen | Japan |
| Drachma | Greece | | | Yuan | China |
| | | | | Zloty | Poland |

# "How come you and Dad went out to dinner and a show but you won't buy me rock concert tickets?"

### *You're tempted to say:*

"Because we earned the money and we can spend it any way we choose."

### *Dr. T's Rx:*

That's the truth, so go ahead and tell it like it is.

As in first question in this chapter, the money itself takes a back seat to the principle: Kids shouldn't be so selfish as to presume that they always get first dibs on the family's resources. You don't need to justify your actions to your children, but it doesn't hurt to remind them that your family's income has to be divided among lots of different expenditures, one of which is R&R for Mom and Dad. You might also remind the child that while you may not choose to buy concert tickets, you *did* spring for an electric guitar (or whatever) on his birthday. Then go off for your night on the town.

In the future, you can head off this question by making concert tickets and other expenses part of your children's budget, to be paid for out of their own allowance or earnings.

*Calvin and Hobbes © 1995 Watterson. Dist. by Universal Press Syndicate. Reprinted with permission. All rights reserved.*

## "How come you bought David a new jacket and you didn't buy one for me?"

### You're tempted to say:

"Because we like David better than we like you."

### Dr. T's Rx:

Actually, that's not a bad comeback—assuming it isn't true and you're smiling while you say it. Meeting your child's unspoken criticism head-on with a little humor can defuse the tension and give you a chance to explain that you intend to buy your whole family new jackets eventually, but you just happened to find one in David's size that was on sale.

Children are sensitive to what they perceive to be favoritism, whether real or imagined (and let's hope it's usually imagined). To the extent it's possible, follow the one-for-all rule: When you buy something for one of your children, buy one for all of them. That's easy enough to do with small items— books from the bookstore, treats at the dollar store, even souvenirs if you go on a business trip (save the bags of peanuts from the plane or the good-night mints on the pillow in your hotel room). A little extra money buys a lot of good will.

If you're going to be shopping for back-to-school clothes and you don't want to take all the kids along at once, let them know that they'll each have a turn. If you're buying a new ball for your young basketball player, it isn't unreasonable to consider a new glove for your baseball player. Of course, if she doesn't need a new glove there's no reason to spend the money. But as long as you've created an overall atmosphere of fairness, she won't feel slighted.

When children complain that you're playing favorites, at least stop and look back over your behav-

*Children are sensitive to what they perceive to be favoritism, whether real or imagined (and let's hope it's usually imagined).*

*It may seem that all your children want to do is spend your money, but often they do worry about whether your family has enough.*

ior. Sometimes the kids aren't imagining things. In blended families, for instance, one spouse sometimes shows financial favoritism toward his or her own children. Grandparents and other family members can be guilty as well.

Bringing things back into balance doesn't have to cost much money. When one woman remarried, she recalls that her new mother-in-law "opened her arms to my two daughters. My kids got birthday cards and valentines just like her own grandchildren did. They got checks, too. The checks were smaller, but the kids were never forgotten. It's not the amount but the thought."

## "Kids cost too much. I'm not going to have any when I grow up."

### Dr. T's Rx:

This isn't exactly a question, but it does demand a response. Somewhere along the line, your kids got the idea (incorrect, Dr. T hopes) that they're undesirable. Tell them that the rewards of having children far outweigh the expense.

Remember that talking *to* your children about money will set them straight about what it can and can't buy, but talking about money over their heads as if they weren't there can give them some cockeyed notions. It may seem that all your children want to do is spend your money, but often they do worry about whether your family has enough:

- Six-year-old Caitlin forgot to return a book to the school library and was told by her teacher that she would have to pay a 10-cent fine. Downcast, Caitlin muttered to herself, "There goes my college fund."

- Watching her mother write a $65 check for a month's worth of piano lessons, 10-year-old Michele looked soberly at her mom and asked, "Can we afford this?"

• A fifth-grade teacher arranged a special field trip for her class to a nearby aquarium. When she told her students that it would cost $12 each, several of them came up to her and told her that the trip was too expensive and they probably wouldn't be able to go.

It's true that money is tight in many households. But in these cases it's likely that the kids' fears were out of proportion to the costs involved. That's not unusual, since children aren't always clear on the difference between $65, $650 or $6,500. One woman recalls that when she was in second grade she was "overwhelmed by the abundance of crayons, stars, paper and pencils in my teacher's supply cabinet. I couldn't imagine that my parents could ever afford to buy me those kinds of things. So I took a bunch."

Kids need to develop a sense of relative costs and values, so that they know which expenses might be expected to fit into your budget and which would be a stretch. In the case of the piano lessons, for example, the mom could have explained that music lessons are a worthwhile expense, and $65 a reasonable cost. But if the child also wanted to take dancing lessons for $65 a month, she might have to choose between the two.

Kids also need to know that they're not a burden but a responsibility that parents (presumably) have taken on willingly. So watch those quips about how paying for braces is going to put you in the poorhouse.

Government statisticians routinely calculate the cost of raising a child from birth to age 18. The latest figure: around $136,000 (not including college), for families with incomes ranging from $32,800 to $55,500. Parents often read the number, shake their heads and sigh, "If I had only known . . ." But even if you had known, you probably would have gone ahead and done it anyway.

*Watch those quips about how paying for braces is going to put you in the poorhouse.*

## **"When we go to visit Mom on weekends, she always buys us neat stuff and takes us places. Why don't you?"**

(Addressed to the custodial parent)

### *You're tempted to say:*

"Because she has all the money and is trying to buy you off."

### *Dr. T's Rx:*

Criticizing your ex-spouse isn't going to work. Whatever bitterness exists between the two of you, your children will resist taking sides (although they're not above trying to exploit the situation to their advantage; see the following question). "In a way, putting down the other parent is like putting down the child," says one family counselor.

Instead of going off on a tirade against your ex-spouse, tell your children that since the divorce your financial circumstances have changed, and that paying for day-to-day expenses doesn't allow a lot of

## For Further Reading

For parents who are dealing with divorces, struggling to stay together, or entering a new marriage, here's a sampling of helpful resources:

### Books

- *Divorce Busting,* by Michele Weiner-Davis (Simon & Schuster, $11)

- *Smart Ways to Save Money During & After Divorce,* by Victoria Collins and Ginita Wall (Nolo Press, $15)

- *Divorce Help Sourcebook,* by Margorie Engel (Visible Ink Press, $17.95)

### Organizations

- **Stepfamily Association of America, 215 Centennial Mall South,** Suite 212, Lincoln, NE, 68508, 800–735–0329

- **Academy of Family Mediators,** 4 Militia Drive, Lexington, MA 02173; 617–674–2663

- **Children of Separation and Divorce Center,** 2000 Century Plaza, Suite 121, Columbia, MD 21044; 410–740–9553 room for extras. Kids sometimes have short memories, and may need a gentle reminder of the little extras you have purchased recently.

Also explain to your child that parents have different ways of showing their love, and the absent spouse may simply be trying to make up for the time he or she doesn't get to spend with the kids. It may leave you gritting your teeth, but when talking to your kids you can afford to be generous to your ex-spouse. If you really have a beef with your ex, you should discuss it with him or her, *not* with the kids. And if he or she really *is* trying to buy off the children, they'll eventually pick up on that themselves. Counselors agree that children learn that a "real" parent is one who makes sure they brush their teeth, helps with homework and offers love and guidance—which can be both of you.

For children, the financial effects of divorce aren't always negative. As long as they're not burdened with the family's financial problems, they can be creative and responsible in finding ways to earn money and save up for the things they want to buy.

"**Before you decide which parent to live with, meet Mr. Winky, who is setting up shop in my backyard.**"

*Reprinted by permission of Andrew Toos*

*To avoid being caught short by unexpected child-related expenses, it helps to write into your divorce settlement a spending plan for the children and a provision to review it periodically.*

## **"I need money for a class trip, and Mom says she doesn't have any. Can I have $20?"**

(Addressed to the noncustodial parent)

### *You're tempted to say:*

"I send your mother money every month. What does she do with it?"

### *Dr. T's Rx:*

See the preceding question. Criticizing your ex-spouse won't score any points with your kids, who may be trying to exploit the tension between the two of you to double dip.

On the other hand, your ex-spouse may really be short on cash. In either case, it's an issue to be resolved between the two adults. Tell your child you'll have to check with the other parent first. You may find out that the $20 for the class trip was supposed to come out of your child's allowance, which he or she spent instead on a new shirt.

Dr. T once received this letter from the divorced father of a teenage son, who lived with his mother some distance away: "My ex-wife told me she had given our son $200 toward books for college, but when he came to visit me he admitted he had spent the money on CDs and asked me for more. He had to have books, so I gave him another $200. I always feel pressured to give him money, but it's easy to get extravagant when I only see him once in a while and I have to compress years into days." The father would save himself both heartache and money by telling his ex-wife in advance that he's willing to pay for school books or other expenses. She would probably appreciate the financial help, and he'd get the satisfaction of spending money on his son.

To avoid being caught short by unexpected child-related expenses, it helps to write into your divorce settlement a spending plan for the children and a provision to review it periodically. Who, for example, is going to pay for class trips, eyeglasses, summer camp, music lessons, special tutoring for slow learners or accelerated programs for gifted ones? If parents have unequal incomes, one might provide money and the other time, with one paying for camp and the other driving there, for example.

Another way to avoid fights about who pays for what is to arrange for both spouses to share more or less equally in child support. Under one system, both parents could draw up a budget for their children's expenses and open a special checking account, funded proportionately based on both their incomes. The checkbook goes back and forth with the kids, and both parents are responsible for handling expenses.

A system like this assumes that ex-spouses are still on speaking terms. In fact, family counselors recommend that parents make it a point to communicate regularly about their kids, even if it's just a phone conversation. "Make a list of the things you're going to talk about, and stick to it," advises one counselor. "If one of you deviates, the other can hang up."

If hang-ups become the rule, you might seek the services of a divorce mediator. As a result of mediation, one couple reached a written agreement that they and their teenage daughter would discuss extraordinary expenses. "The three of us would decide who could do what, and whether the thing should be bought in the first place," says the father. "We paid the mediator $900 to settle something $75,000 in legal fees hadn't settled."

You and your spouse may have split up, but you're both still parents with a common interest in how money is spent on your kids. Getting involved in a bidding war is a lose-lose-lose situation. Instead, ask yourselves how you'd handle the situation if you were still together.

*Another way to avoid fights about who pays for what is to arrange for both spouses to share more or less equally in child support.*

For parents of minor children, the single most important reason for making a will is to name a guardian for the kids.

# "Who will take care of us if you die?"

### You're tempted to say:
"That's all been arranged."

### Dr. T's Rx:

Nothing is really wrong with that answer—assuming it's true. But it would be even better if you told your kids whom you have named as their guardians should anything happen to you. And if you haven't named any guardians, your child's question should be the encouragement you need.

Many parents rely on informal arrangements—"My wife's sister has agreed to take care of our children in case my wife and I die." But if both you and your spouse should die before your children are grown without formally naming a guardian, the courts will decide who's going to bring up your kids. And you can't count on your wishes being honored. A judge who doesn't know your children and family could choose the one relative you *wouldn't* want.

Suppose you feel that your sister would be the ideal guardian for your children, but your husband's brother thinks he'd be an even better one. In the absence of a will naming one or the other, both could make a claim and a nasty court fight could ensue. Moreover, the cost of the battle would come out of your estate—that is, your kids' pockets.

In fact, for parents of minor children the single most important reason for making a will is to name a guardian for the kids. Many parents put off writing a will because they see it as a downer—a way to dispose of your assets after death. Think of it instead as a way to protect your *most precious* assets.

In your will you can name both a guardian of the person—someone who shares your family values and philosophy of child-rearing—and a guardian of the property—someone with financial acumen to manage your children's inheritance. It could be the same person if you can settle on someone who shares your values and is financially astute. Before naming anyone, discuss with the candidates whether they're willing to do the job. If your children are old enough, ask them for their observations. And always name a backup. Review your choices if you have additional children, if your guardian should move away, or if your financial circumstances change.

Even guardians may be required to report to the court on how they're spending your children's assets. It's smart to take the extra step of setting up a trust to be the beneficiary of any property you leave your children. Don't discount the value of your assets, or think that trusts are only for "rich" people (of whom you're certainly not one). Even if you own only a house and an insurance policy, your children could come into a chunk of money. And your assets will probably grow over the years.

A trust avoids court supervision of those assets. It also lets you specify how the income and principal should be used, and at what age you want the principal to be distributed to your children. In short, it gives you a perpetual say in how your children will be raised—which should be reassuring to you as well as to them.

# Dr. T's Final Rx

**P**oliticians and the media are obsessed with family values. Bookstore shelves are crammed with volumes advising your family how to acquire them. Americans, it seems, are on a crusade to find stability and set standards.

Inevitably those standards are going to involve money, because many of the values and virtues we want to pass along to our children touch on finances either directly or indirectly–thrift, self-discipline, generosity, responsibility, planning for the future. If children acquire those traits in the context of managing money successfully, they'll be able to use them to manage other aspects of their lives as well.

But no one can give you a secret formula for achieving family harmony or financial balance. The answer is within the grasp of any family. It's a matter of common-sense principles effectively communicated to your children. In the case of money, those principles include living within your means and recognizing virtue as its own reward. That so many families struggle with principles that seem so obvious is a sign of modern times, when outside influences and affluence can upset the delicate balance of family life.

Dr. T's contribution is to offer suggestions on how to counter those outside influences. Some parents are already doing a great job and just need a pat on the back and a word of encouragement. Others have lost sight of basic values and need guidance about how to get back on track. Still others know exactly what they want to teach their children but are looking for practical suggestions on how to discuss sensitive issues involving money or answer awkward questions.

*Mom, Can I Have That?* has tried to provide the pat on the back, the gentle reminder, the practical advice. Back in Chapter One, Dr. T observed that when children ask their parents about money, parents are tempted to offer one of three responses: Yes, no or maybe. Here, in a nutshell, is Dr. T's prescription for answering those questions more effectively:

- **Never say no unless you mean it.**

- **Never say yes unless you want to.**

- **Never say maybe if you can think of a better response –and, having read this book, you can.**

### Dr. T wants to hear from you

If you have any comments or questions for Dr. T, write to Janet Bodnar, 1729 H Street, N.W., Washington, DC, 20006, or e-mail Ask Dr T@aol.com.